WTF is Crypto?

A Step-by-Step Guide for Beginners.

Jason Ansell

Copyright @2024 WTF is Crypto

ALL RIGHT RESERVED

All rights reserved. No part of this publication may be reproduced, stored in a retrieved system, or transmitted in any form or by any means electronic, mechanical, photocopying, recording or otherwise, without the prior permission of the author.

Table of Contents

Introduction Welcome to the World of Crypto 1

Chapter 1: 7
What is Cryptocurrency? 7

Chapter 1.1: 15
What Makes Cryptocurrency Different? 15

Chapter 1.2: 24
The Basics of Blockchain Technology 24

Chapter 1.3: 35
Why Are There So Many Cryptocurrencies? 35

Chapter 1.4: 47
Key Terminology What You Need to Know 47

Chapter 1.5: 64
Why Cryptocurrency Matters 64

Chapter 1.6: 76
Bringing It Home 76

Chapter 2: 81
Getting Started with Wallets 81

Chapter 3: 93

How to Buy Your First Cryptocurrency.. 93

Chapter 4: 105

Building a Beginner's Portfolio.. 105

Chapter 5: 119

Staying Safe in the Crypto World 119

Chapter 6: 134

Exploring Use Cases... 134

Chapter 7:...150

Understanding Trends in Crypto 150

Chapter 8: 167

Taking Your First Steps 167

Chapter 9: 178

Your Journey Forward 178

Bonus Material: 189

Motivation For Your Mission.. 189

Introduction
Welcome to the World of Crypto

Your Journey Starts Here

Welcome to the fascinating world of cryptocurrency and blockchain—a world that is transforming how we think about money, technology, and even trust itself. If you're reading this, chances are you've heard the buzz about Bitcoin, Ethereum, or NFTs, and you're curious about how it all works. Maybe you're looking to invest, or perhaps you're just eager to understand what all the excitement is about. Whatever your motivation, you've come to the right place.

This book is your guide to unlocking the potential of this revolutionary technology. We'll explore the fundamental concepts, the underlying technology, and the practical applications that are shaping the future of finance and beyond. From the early days of Bitcoin to the latest advancements in DeFi and NFTs, we'll cover it all in an easy-to-understand manner.

Whether you're a tech-savvy enthusiast or a complete beginner, this book is designed to empower you with the knowledge and tools you need to navigate the dynamic world of cryptocurrency. Join us on this exciting journey as we uncover the secrets behind this groundbreaking technology and explore the limitless possibilities it holds.

Who Am I?

Let me start by introducing myself. My name is **Jason Ansell**, and I've spent the better part of two decades working in technology, digital marketing, and blockchain development. I'm a **self-taught full-stack developer** and an entrepreneur who thrives on creating, building, and solving complex problems. Over the years, I've had the privilege of working on a wide range of projects—from digital marketing campaigns for local businesses to founding and scaling blockchain platforms like **Vector Smart Chain (VSC)**.

I wear many hats in this ever-evolving crypto landscape:

- **As a Project Founder**, I've experienced firsthand what it takes to launch and scale blockchain projects. I've helped build ecosystems from the ground up, navigating the challenges and opportunities that come with pioneering new technology.

- **As a Developer**, I've written smart contracts, designed decentralized applications (dApps), and worked on Layer-1 blockchain solutions. I understand the nuts and bolts of what makes blockchain technology tick and how it can be applied to solve real-world problems.

- **As an Investor,** I've explored the crypto market from an analytical perspective, learning how to identify promising projects and manage risks. My journey has included both successes and lessons learned—experiences I'm eager to share with you.

Why I Wrote This Book

I wrote this book because I understand how overwhelming the crypto space can feel when you're just starting. I've met countless people—friends, colleagues, and community members—who wanted to dive into crypto but didn't know where to begin. With so much jargon, complex technology, and a constant stream of news, it's easy to feel lost.

This book is my way of cutting through the noise. I want to give you a clear, actionable roadmap to help you take your first steps with confidence. Whether you're setting up your first wallet, buying your first Bitcoin, or simply trying to understand how blockchain works, this guide will walk you through it all.

I'm passionate about making the world of crypto accessible to everyone. My goal is to demystify the complex concepts, provide practical advice, and inspire you to explore the exciting opportunities that this technology offers. By the end of this book, you'll have a solid foundation of knowledge and the tools to navigate the crypto landscape with ease. Let's embark on this journey together!

Why Should You Care About Crypto?

The truth is, cryptocurrency isn't just a passing trend—it's a revolution. It's changing how we:

- **Think about money:** With crypto, you can send value anywhere in the world instantly, without intermediaries like banks. This can lead to greater financial inclusion for people around the globe.
- **Interact with technology:** Blockchain isn't just about money; it's about creating decentralized systems that empower people. From supply chain management to voting systems, blockchain technology can improve transparency, security, and efficiency.
- **Build communities:** Crypto enables new ways of organizing, collaborating, and even governing through tools like DAOs (Decentralized Autonomous Organizations). These decentralized organizations allow communities to make decisions collectively, without the need for traditional hierarchies.

Cryptocurrency is reshaping industries from finance to art, and we're only scratching the surface of what's possible. Whether you're here to invest, build, or simply learn, there's a place for you in this space. By understanding the fundamentals of cryptocurrency and blockchain, you can position yourself to take advantage of the opportunities that lie ahead.

What You'll Learn

This book is designed to guide you through the essentials:

- **Understanding what cryptocurrency and blockchain technology are:** We'll delve into the fundamental concepts, explaining how these technologies work and why they're revolutionizing various industries.
- **Setting up your first wallet and buying your first crypto:** We'll walk you through the step-by-step process of creating a secure wallet and purchasing your first cryptocurrency.
- **Staying safe and avoiding common pitfalls:** We'll discuss essential security practices, such as protecting your private keys and identifying common scams.
- **Exploring the exciting use cases and trends shaping the future of crypto:** We'll explore the potential of decentralized finance (DeFi), non-fungible tokens (NFTs), and other innovative applications of blockchain technology.

I'll be sharing not just facts and definitions but also personal stories, lessons learned, and insights gained from my journey as a founder, developer, and investor. By combining technical knowledge with real-world experience, I aim to provide a comprehensive and engaging learning experience.

A Word of Encouragement

Finally, I want to leave you with this: entering the crypto space is like learning a new language. It might feel confusing at first, but with patience and persistence, it starts to make sense—and before you know it, you're fluent. Don't worry if you're starting from zero; we all did at one point.

Remember, the crypto world is constantly evolving. What may be true today might change tomorrow. Stay curious, keep learning, and embrace the exciting journey ahead.

By the time you finish this book, you'll have a solid foundation to navigate the world of crypto confidently. You'll also be equipped with the tools and knowledge to take your first steps—and maybe even help shape the future of this exciting technology.

So, let's get started. Welcome to your first crypto journey.

The future is waiting!

Chapter 1:

What is Cryptocurrency?

The Evolution of Money: From Barter to Blockchain

To understand cryptocurrency, we first need to look at how money itself has evolved. Thousands of years ago, people traded goods and services through bartering. If a farmer needed shoes, they'd trade eggs with the cobbler. Barter worked—until it didn't. The problem was that it relied on a coincidence of wants: both parties had to want what the other was offering at the same time.

Enter money. First, it was shells and beads, then precious metals like gold and silver. These physical forms of money were more portable and divisible than goods, making trade more efficient. However, they were still subject to theft, damage, and the limitations of physical transportation.

Eventually, paper money emerged, followed by digital payments. These innovations further streamlined trade, reducing the need for physical currency and enabling transactions to occur across vast distances. However, these systems still relied on centralized institutions, such as banks, to process and verify transactions.

Cryptocurrency is the next step in this evolution. It's money designed for the internet age: digital, decentralized, and powered by groundbreaking technology called blockchain. By leveraging the power of cryptography and distributed networks, cryptocurrencies offer a new paradigm for finance, promising greater security, transparency, and accessibility.

The Barter System: The First Form of Trade

Bartering was humanity's earliest method of trade, where goods and services were exchanged directly. While it worked for small, localized economies, it came with significant limitations:

- **Inefficiency:** Finding someone who both had what you wanted and wanted what you had was a challenge. This often led to time-consuming and inefficient processes.
- **Lack of Standardization:** The value of goods was subjective and could vary depending on individual needs and preferences. How many chickens were a cow worth? It depended on who you asked and the specific circumstances of the trade.
- **Non-Divisibility:** Some goods couldn't be divided into smaller units for trade. You couldn't exactly give someone half a cow. This limitation made it difficult to facilitate transactions involving smaller amounts of valu

Despite these drawbacks, bartering laid the foundation for the concept of exchanging value. It demonstrated the fundamental human desire to trade and the need for a more efficient system

The Birth of Money

To overcome the inefficiencies of bartering, societies developed money as a medium of exchange. It went through several evolutionary stages:

Commodity Money: Items like shells, salt, or precious metals became the first forms of money. These items were chosen because they were widely accepted, durable, and had intrinsic value. However, commodity money was often bulky, difficult to transport, and susceptible to fluctuations in value based on supply and demand.

Metal Money: Gold and silver coins became standard currencies due to their portability, divisibility, and inherent worth. Early coins were stamped by rulers to verify authenticity and weight. Metal money provided a more standardized and reliable medium of exchange, reducing the uncertainties associated with bartering.

Paper Money: Paper currency was first introduced in China during the Tang Dynasty (618–907 CE) and became widely used during the Song Dynasty. In Europe, banks began issuing notes backed by gold or silver reserves, marking the start of the gold standard. Paper money offered greater convenience and portability than metal coins, but it was still tied to the value of physical assets.

Fiat Money: Today, most money is fiat, meaning it has no intrinsic value but is backed by the trust and authority of governments. Fiat money allows governments to control the economy through monetary policy, such as printing money or adjusting interest rates. However, it's susceptible to inflation and devaluation, which can erode the purchasing power of money over time.

The Digital Revolution

The internet era brought a new evolution in money:

Electronic Money:

- Debit and credit cards, online banking, and payment systems like PayPal digitized fiat money.
- These systems rely on centralized institutions like banks and payment processors to verify and clear transactions.
- While they offer convenience and speed, they are still subject to the limitations of traditional finance, such as high fees, slow processing times, and limited access for unbanked populations.

Mobile Payments:

- Platforms like Apple Pay, Google Wallet, and Alipay made transactions even more convenient, allowing users to make payments with their smartphones.
- However, they still operate within the traditional financial system, relying on banks and payment processors to facilitate transactions.

While digital payments improved efficiency, they didn't solve fundamental issues like high fees, exclusion of unbanked populations, and reliance on centralized entities. The need for a more efficient, inclusive, and secure financial system persisted.

Enter Cryptocurrency: Money for the Internet Age

In 2009, Bitcoin emerged as the world's first cryptocurrency. Unlike fiat or electronic money, Bitcoin offered:

- **Decentralization:** No central authority or government controls it. This means that Bitcoin is resistant to censorship and manipulation by governments or financial institutions.
- **Borderlessness:** Bitcoin transactions can happen anywhere, anytime, without intermediaries. This enables fast, cheap, and global transfers of value.
- **Limited Supply:** Bitcoin's total supply is capped at 21 million coins, making it immune to inflation caused by overprinting. This scarcity ensures that Bitcoin's value can appreciate over time.

Cryptocurrency represents a paradigm shift:

- **Digital:** It exists entirely in cyberspace. This makes it more efficient and secure than physical currency.
- **Secure:** Blockchain technology ensures transactions are tamper-proof and transparent. This provides a high level of security and trust.
- **Inclusive:** Anyone with internet access can participate, even in regions with limited banking infrastructure. This

can empower individuals and promote financial inclusion.

By combining these features, cryptocurrencies offer a new vision for the future of finance, promising greater financial freedom, transparency, and security for all.

Blockchain: The Backbone of Cryptocurrency

Cryptocurrency wouldn't exist without blockchain technology. The blockchain:

- **Solves the double-spending problem:** In traditional digital systems, it's easy to copy and paste digital assets, leading to the risk of double-spending. Blockchain solves this problem by creating a distributed ledger where each transaction is recorded and verified by a network of computers. This makes it impossible for anyone to spend the same asset twice.
- **Acts as a public ledger:** The blockchain is a public record of all transactions, accessible to anyone. This transparency and immutability create trust in a trustless environment, as all participants can verify the authenticity of transactions.
- **Enables the creation of decentralized applications (dApps) and smart contracts:** Blockchain technology can power a new generation of applications that are decentralized, transparent, and resistant to censorship. Smart contracts, self-executing contracts with the terms

of the agreement directly written into code, can automate processes and reduce the need for intermediaries.

By providing a secure, transparent, and decentralized foundation, blockchain technology is revolutionizing various industries, from finance to supply chain management and beyond.

Why This Evolution Matters

The journey from barter to blockchain reflects humanity's constant push for better ways to trade and exchange value. Each step in this evolution solved the problems of the era before it. Cryptocurrency and blockchain are not just the next step—they're a leap forward.

For individuals:

- **Financial Empowerment:** Cryptocurrency puts power back in your hands. No bank fees, no intermediaries—just you and your money. You can send and receive funds globally, quickly, and at a fraction of the cost of traditional methods.
- **Privacy and Security:** Blockchain technology offers a high level of security and privacy, protecting your financial information from potential hacks and fraud.
- **Financial Inclusion:** Cryptocurrencies can provide access to financial services for billions of people who are unbanked or underbanked.

For businesses:

- **Efficiency and Transparency:** Blockchain technology can streamline supply chains, reduce fraud, and improve transparency in various industries.
- **Innovation and New Business Models:** Cryptocurrencies and blockchain enable the creation of innovative business models and decentralized applications that can disrupt traditional industries.

For the world:

- **Financial Inclusion:** By providing access to financial services for billions of people, cryptocurrency can help alleviate poverty and promote economic growth.
- **Transparency and Accountability:** Blockchain technology can increase transparency and accountability in government, healthcare, and other sectors.
- **Global Economic Cooperation:** Cryptocurrency can facilitate cross-border transactions and reduce the reliance on traditional financial systems, promoting global economic cooperation.

The future of finance and technology is being shaped by the power of cryptocurrency and blockchain. By understanding these technologies and their potential, we can position ourselves to benefit from the opportunities they offer.

Chapter 1.1

What Makes Cryptocurrency Different?

At its core, cryptocurrency is a form of digital currency that exists only online. But unlike traditional money, it doesn't rely on banks or governments to work. Instead, it uses blockchain technology—a decentralized, transparent system where every transaction is recorded.

Here are three key features that set cryptocurrency apart:

Decentralization: No single entity, like a bank or government, controls cryptocurrencies. Instead, they run on networks of computers around the world.

Transparency: Every transaction is recorded on a public ledger (the blockchain) that anyone can view. This transparency builds trust.

Security: Transactions are encrypted and irreversible, reducing fraud and chargebacks.

Cryptocurrency isn't just digital money—it's a groundbreaking innovation that changes how we think about value, trust, and ownership. Here, we'll dive deeper into the features that set cryptocurrency apart and explore why these distinctions matter.

1. Decentralization: Breaking Free from Central Authority

Most traditional currencies, like the US dollar or euro, are controlled by central authorities such as governments and central banks. These entities regulate supply, oversee transactions, and maintain trust in the system. However, this centralization comes with drawbacks:

- Vulnerability to corruption and inefficiency.
- Risks of inflation due to overprinting money.
- Dependence on intermediaries like banks, which charge fees and impose restrictions.

Cryptocurrency flips this model on its head.

- It operates on decentralized networks of computers (nodes) that work together to validate and record transactions.
- There's no central entity to control or manipulate the currency.

Why It Matters:

- You own your money. No government can freeze your account or devalue your savings through inflation.

- Transactions are resistant to censorship. No one can stop or block your payments.

Real-World Example: In countries facing economic instability, like Venezuela, cryptocurrencies like Bitcoin offer a lifeline by providing an alternative to unstable fiat currencies.

2. Transparency: A Trustless System You Can Trust

Traditional financial systems rely on trust in intermediaries like banks or payment processors. If you transfer money, you trust the bank to process it accurately and honestly. However, this trust can be misplaced—think bank errors, fraud, or corruption.

Cryptocurrency replaces trust with transparency.

- Every transaction is recorded on a public ledger called the blockchain.
- Anyone can view the blockchain to verify transactions.
- Cryptographic algorithms ensure the data's integrity, making it nearly impossible to tamper with.

Why It Matters:

- Greater accountability. Transparent systems reduce fraud and corruption.
- Equal access. You don't need to trust a third party—just the blockchain.

Real-World Example: Ethereum's blockchain is often used to create smart contracts—agreements that automatically execute once conditions are met. These contracts remove the need for middlemen, ensuring fairness and transparency.

3. Security: Protecting Your Assets

Digital transactions in traditional systems are prone to fraud and hacking. Credit card numbers can be stolen, and online accounts can be compromised. Cryptocurrency takes a different approach to security.

Cryptocurrency is secured by cryptography.

- Transactions are verified by solving complex mathematical puzzles (proof-of-work) or validating blocks of data (proof-of-stake).
- Once recorded on the blockchain, transactions cannot be altered or deleted.

Additional Security Features:

- **Private Keys**: A unique digital signature that only the owner holds. Without your private key, no one can access your funds.
- **Decentralization**: No single point of failure. Hacking one computer won't compromise the entire network.

Why It Matters:

- Transactions are tamper-proof and immutable.
- Cryptocurrencies reduce fraud and enhance trust in digital transactions.

Real-World Example: The Bitcoin network has never been hacked, demonstrating the robustness of blockchain security.

4. Borderlessness: Money Without Borders

Traditional money is tied to geographic and political boundaries. Sending money across borders often involves:

- **High fees:** Banks and financial institutions charge significant fees for international transfers.
- **Long delays:** Cross-border transactions can take several days to process.
- **Currency conversion complexities:** Exchanging currencies can involve additional fees and exchange rate fluctuations.

Cryptocurrency removes these barriers.

- **It operates on the internet, making it accessible worldwide.** This means that cryptocurrency transactions can occur between any two points on the globe, regardless of geographical location.
- **Transactions happen instantly, regardless of where the sender and receiver are located.** This enables fast and efficient transfers of value, without the delays associated with traditional banking systems.
- **No need for currency conversion when using globally recognized cryptocurrencies like Bitcoin or stablecoins like USDT.** This simplifies cross-border transactions and eliminates the need for currency exchange fees.

Why It Matters:

- **Facilitates global commerce:** By removing barriers to international trade, cryptocurrency can promote economic growth and development.
- **Empowers individuals in countries with restrictive financial systems:** Cryptocurrency can provide access to financial services for people who are unbanked or underbanked, empowering them to participate in the global economy.

Real-World Example: Millions of migrant workers use cryptocurrencies to send money home, bypassing high fees from traditional remittance services. This allows them to support their families more efficiently and cost-effectively.

5. Limited Supply: Protecting Against Inflation

Governments can print unlimited amounts of fiat money, leading to inflation and reduced purchasing power. In contrast:

- **Many cryptocurrencies, like Bitcoin, have a fixed supply cap.** For Bitcoin, this is 21 million coins. This means that no new Bitcoin will ever be created beyond this limit.
- **Others, like Ethereum, control supply through network rules and economic incentives.** This ensures a steady and predictable supply of the cryptocurrency, reducing the risk of inflation.

Why It Matters:

- **Fixed or controlled supply creates scarcity, increasing the value of the asset over time.** As demand for a cryptocurrency increases, and the supply remains fixed or limited, the price of the cryptocurrency tends to rise.
- **Protects against the devaluation of money.** By limiting the supply of cryptocurrency, it can act as a hedge against inflation, preserving the purchasing power of your investment.

Real-World Example: Bitcoin is often referred to as "digital gold" because of its scarcity and its role as a store of value. Just like gold, Bitcoin's limited supply makes it a desirable asset for investors seeking to protect their wealth from inflation and economic uncertainty.

6. Programmability: Money That Thinks

Unlike traditional money, cryptocurrencies can be programmed to perform specific tasks through smart contracts. These are self-executing agreements where the terms of the agreement are directly written into code.

Why It Matters:

- **Enables Decentralized Applications (dApps) and Services:** Smart contracts power a new generation of decentralized applications that operate without intermediaries. This includes DeFi (Decentralized

Finance) platforms, which offer a range of financial services, such as lending, borrowing, and trading, directly on the blockchain.
- **Automates Processes, Reducing Costs and Increasing Efficiency:** Smart contracts can automate various processes, from supply chain management to real estate transactions. By eliminating intermediaries and automating tasks, smart contracts can significantly reduce costs and increase efficiency.
- **Real-World Example:** Decentralized lending platforms like Aave allow users to lend and borrow cryptocurrency directly, without the need for a traditional bank. Smart contracts ensure that the terms of the loan are enforced automatically, eliminating the risk of default and fraud.

Programmability is one of the most powerful features of cryptocurrencies and blockchain technology. It opens up a world of possibilities for innovation and disruption, transforming various industries and empowering individuals.

WTF Does It All Mean?

Cryptocurrency is more than just digital money. It's a revolution that empowers individuals, promotes transparency, enhances security, and removes the inefficiencies of traditional systems. It's not just a new way to pay—it's a new way to think about money and trust in the digital age.

By understanding the fundamentals of cryptocurrency and blockchain technology, you're well-equipped to navigate this exciting and rapidly evolving landscape. Whether you're an investor, a developer, or simply someone curious about the future of finance, this knowledge will empower you to make informed decisions and seize the opportunities that lie ahead.

As you continue your journey into the world of crypto, remember to stay curious, stay informed, and most importantly, stay safe. With the right knowledge and a cautious approach, you can unlock the potential of this transformative technology and shape the future of finance.

Chapter 1.2:

The Basics of Blockchain Technology

Think of blockchain as a digital ledger. Imagine a notebook where every page is a "block" of information. Once a page is full, it's added to a "chain" of pages in chronological order. This is why it's called a blockchain.

Here's what makes it revolutionary:

- **Decentralized:** Instead of being stored in one place (like a bank's server), copies of the blockchain exist on thousands of computers worldwide. This distributed nature makes it highly resistant to censorship and attacks.
- **Immutable:** Once a block is added to the chain, it cannot be changed or erased. This ensures the integrity and security of the data, as it's virtually impossible to alter the history of transactions.
- **Trustless:** Transactions are verified by the network of computers, rather than by a central authority. This eliminates the need for intermediaries, such as banks, making the system more efficient and transparent.

This system ensures security, transparency, and efficiency—qualities that make cryptocurrency possible. By understanding the fundamental principles of blockchain technology, you can appreciate the potential of cryptocurrencies and other decentralized applications.

What is Blockchain?

At its core, blockchain is a digital ledger. Imagine it as a chain of blocks, where each block contains a record of transactions. These blocks are linked together chronologically and secured using cryptographic methods.

But here's the twist: instead of being stored in one central location, like a bank's database, blockchain is decentralized. It's distributed across thousands of computers (nodes) around the world, each holding a copy of the ledger. This distributed nature makes it highly resistant to attacks and censorship.

When a new transaction occurs, it's added to a block. Once the block is filled with transactions, it's added to the chain, and all nodes in the network verify the block's validity. This consensus mechanism ensures that the blockchain remains secure and accurate.

The key features of blockchain technology are:

- **Decentralization:** No single entity controls the network.
- **Immutability:** Once a transaction is recorded, it cannot be altered.

- **Transparency:** All transactions are visible to everyone on the network.
- **Security:** Cryptographic techniques protect the integrity of the blockchain.

These features make blockchain a powerful tool for various applications, from finance to supply chain management and beyond.

How Blockchain Works: A Simple Analogy

Think of blockchain as a shared spreadsheet:

- **The Spreadsheet:** Represents the blockchain ledger, a digital record of transactions.
- **The Rows:** Contain transaction records (e.g., Alice sends Bob 1 Bitcoin). Each row includes information like the sender, receiver, amount, and a timestamp.
- **The Updates:** Every time a transaction happens, a new row is added to the spreadsheet, and every participant gets an updated copy.

What makes it unique is that:

- **No one can alter past rows (transactions) without everyone knowing.** This is because the blockchain is distributed across multiple computers, and any attempt to change a past transaction would require altering the data on all these computers simultaneously, which is practically impossible.

- **Everyone agrees on what's in the spreadsheet through a process called consensus.** Different blockchains use various consensus mechanisms, such as Proof of Work (PoW) and Proof of Stake (PoS), to ensure that all participants agree on the validity of transactions and the state of the blockchain.

This consensus mechanism ensures that the blockchain remains secure, transparent, and reliable. It prevents fraud, double-spending, and other malicious activities.

Key Features of Blockchain

Blockchain technology offers several key features that make it a powerful tool for various applications:

1. **Decentralization:** Instead of relying on a single authority (like a bank), the blockchain is maintained by a network of nodes. Each node holds a copy of the blockchain, ensuring no single point of failure. This decentralized nature makes the blockchain resistant to censorship and attacks, as it would require compromising a significant portion of the network.

2. **Transparency:** All transactions are publicly visible on the blockchain. While transactions are public, the identities behind them remain pseudonymous, protecting user privacy. This transparency allows for greater trust and accountability, as all participants can verify the authenticity of transactions.

3. **Immutability:** Once data is recorded in a block, it cannot be changed or deleted. This ensures that transaction records are permanent and tamper-proof. This immutability makes blockchain a reliable source of truth, as it prevents fraudulent activities and disputes.
4. **Security:** Transactions are encrypted and verified by the network before being added to the blockchain. The decentralized nature of the blockchain makes it resistant to hacking and fraud. The use of cryptographic techniques, such as digital signatures, ensures the security and authenticity of transactions.

These features make blockchain a powerful tool for various applications, from finance to supply chain management and beyond.

A Closer Look at Blocks

Each block in the blockchain contains:

- **Data:** The transaction details (e.g., who sent what to whom, the amount, and any additional data relevant to the transaction).
- **Timestamp:** When the transaction occurred. This timestamp helps to order transactions chronologically and ensures that the blockchain is accurate and consistent.
- **Hash:** A unique digital fingerprint for the block. This hash is generated using a cryptographic algorithm that

takes the block's data as input. Any change to the data, no matter how small, will result in a completely different hash.

- **Previous Block's Hash:** This links the current block to the previous block in the chain, forming an unbroken chain of blocks. This linkage ensures that the order of blocks cannot be altered.

This linking of hashes is what makes blockchain so secure. If someone tries to tamper with a block, its hash changes, breaking the chain and alerting the network. The network would then reject the altered block, maintaining the integrity of the blockchain.

This process, known as proof of work, ensures that the blockchain remains secure and tamper-proof.

Consensus Mechanisms: How Blockchain Stays Honest

Consensus mechanisms ensure that all nodes in the network agree on the validity of transactions. Here are two common methods:

1. **Proof of Work (PoW):**
    - Used by Bitcoin and many other blockchains.
    - Miners solve complex mathematical puzzles to validate transactions and add them to the blockchain.

- The first miner to solve the puzzle adds the block to the chain and is rewarded with cryptocurrency.
- This process requires significant computational power and energy consumption.

2. **Proof of Stake (PoS):**

    - Used by Ethereum 2.0 and other blockchains.
    - Validators are chosen to create new blocks based on the amount of cryptocurrency they "stake" (lock up as collateral).
    - The more cryptocurrency a validator stakes, the higher their chance of being selected to create a block.
    - PoS is generally more energy-efficient than PoW.

By using these consensus mechanisms, blockchains ensure that the network remains secure, reliable, and resistant to attacks.

Applications of Blockchain Technology

Blockchain isn't just for cryptocurrencies. Its unique features enable a wide range of applications:

1. **Cryptocurrency:**

    - The first and most well-known use case (e.g., Bitcoin, Ethereum).

- Cryptocurrencies offer a decentralized and secure way to transfer value, enabling financial inclusion and global transactions.

2. Smart Contracts:

- Self-executing agreements where the terms are written into code.
- Smart contracts can automate processes, reducing the need for intermediaries and ensuring transparency and trust.
- Example: Automatically releasing payment when goods are delivered, ensuring that the payment is only released once the goods are received and verified.

3. Supply Chain Management:

- Tracking goods from production to delivery for greater transparency and efficiency.
- By recording the origin, transit, and ownership of products on the blockchain, businesses can reduce fraud, counterfeiting, and supply chain disruptions.
- Example: Ensuring the authenticity of products like diamonds or organic food by tracking their journey from source to consumer.

4. Decentralized Finance (DeFi):

- Financial services like lending, borrowing, and trading without intermediaries.
- DeFi platforms leverage blockchain technology to create peer-to-peer financial systems, offering greater accessibility and lower fees.
- Example: Platforms like Uniswap and Aave allow users to trade and lend cryptocurrency directly, without the need for traditional financial institutions.

5. **Identity Verification:**

    - Securely storing and managing personal data for digital IDs.
    - Blockchain-based digital identities can be more secure and privacy-preserving than traditional methods.
    - Example: Blockchain-based digital passports can be used to verify identity and facilitate travel.

As blockchain technology continues to evolve, we can expect to see even more innovative applications emerge, transforming various industries and reshaping the future of technology.

Why Blockchain Matters

Blockchain is more than just a database; it's a tool that redefines trust in the digital world. Here's why it's important:

- **Trustless Transactions:** Blockchain enables trustless transactions, meaning that individuals can interact with each other directly without the need for intermediaries like banks or payment processors. This reduces transaction costs, speeds up processes, and empowers individuals to take control of their finances.
- **Global Accessibility:** Blockchain technology is accessible to anyone with an internet connection, regardless of their geographical location. This fosters financial inclusion and enables cross-border transactions without the limitations of traditional banking systems.
- **Security and Reliability:** The decentralized nature of blockchain and the use of cryptographic techniques ensure that transactions are secure, transparent, and tamper-proof. This helps to prevent fraud, reduce errors, and increase trust in digital systems.

By leveraging the power of blockchain, we can build a more efficient, transparent, and secure digital future.

WTF Does It All Mean?

Blockchain is the foundation that makes cryptocurrency possible. Without it, digital money wouldn't be secure, decentralized, or transparent. Understanding how blockchain works is the first step to appreciating the full potential of cryptocurrencies and the new systems they enable.

By grasping the concepts of decentralization, immutability, and consensus mechanisms, you can unlock the power of blockchain and its applications. This knowledge will empower you to make informed decisions, navigate the complex world of cryptocurrencies, and participate in the digital revolution.

Pro Tip: Blockchain may seem complex at first, but at its heart, it's just a way to store and share information securely. The more you explore it, the clearer it becomes. Don't be afraid to experiment, ask questions, and join online communities to learn from others. By taking the time to understand the underlying technology, you'll be better equipped to harness its potential and shape the future.

Chapter 1.3:

Why Are There So Many Cryptocurrencies?

When Bitcoin was created in 2009, by an anonymous person (or group) using the pseudonym *Satoshi Nakamoto*. It was the world's first cryptocurrency designed as a decentralized alternative to traditional money and remains the most well-known. But today, there are thousands of cryptocurrencies, each with its unique purpose, features, and ecosystem.

Since then, thousands of cryptocurrencies have been created, each with its own purpose. Here are a few examples:

- **Bitcoin (BTC):** The original cryptocurrency, often referred to as "digital gold."
- **Ethereum (ETH):** A platform for building decentralized applications (dApps) using smart contracts.
- **Stablecoins:** Cryptocurrencies pegged to traditional currencies like the US dollar, designed to reduce volatility.
- **Altcoins:** Any cryptocurrency that isn't Bitcoin, such as Solana (SOL) or Vector Smart Gas (VSG).

Each cryptocurrency serves different use cases, from payments to creating digital economies for apps and games. Let's explore why the crypto space has grown so much and what differentiates these digital assets.

1. Bitcoin: The Pioneer and Digital Gold

Bitcoin was designed to solve one specific problem: creating a decentralized, peer-to-peer digital currency that doesn't rely on governments or banks. It set the foundation for the cryptocurrency revolution by introducing:

- **Decentralization:** Transactions are verified by the network of miners, rather than a central authority. This makes Bitcoin resistant to censorship and manipulation.
- **Scarcity:** A fixed supply of 21 million coins ensures that Bitcoin's value is protected from inflation.
- **Security:** Transactions are recorded on an immutable blockchain, making them secure and transparent.

Why It's Unique:

Bitcoin is often called "digital gold" because, like gold, it's seen as a store of value. Its limited supply and decentralized nature make it a desirable asset for investors seeking to protect their wealth. However, Bitcoin's design limits its use as a platform for building decentralized applications. Its slow transaction speeds and high fees make it less suitable for everyday transactions.

2. Ethereum: The Programmable Blockchain

In 2015, Ethereum took blockchain technology to the next level by introducing smart contracts—self-executing programs that run on the blockchain. This innovation made it possible to build decentralized applications (dApps) for purposes beyond simple transactions.

Why Ethereum Matters:

- **Programmability:** Ethereum's smart contract functionality allows developers to create a wide range of decentralized applications, from financial services to supply chain management and gaming.
- **Widespread Adoption:** Ethereum's blockchain hosts thousands of tokens and dApps, making it the most popular and widely used blockchain platform.
- **Scalability:** While Ethereum has faced scalability challenges in the past, ongoing developments like Ethereum 2.0 aim to address these issues and improve the network's performance.

Examples:

- **Uniswap:** A decentralized exchange that allows users to trade cryptocurrencies directly with each other without the need for intermediaries.
- **OpenSea:** An NFT marketplace where users can buy, sell, and trade non-fungible tokens representing unique digital assets.

Ethereum has revolutionized the blockchain industry by demonstrating the potential of smart contracts and decentralized applications. As the technology continues to evolve, Ethereum is poised to play a crucial role in shaping the future of the internet.

3. Altcoins: Beyond Bitcoin and Ethereum

The term "altcoin" refers to any cryptocurrency that isn't Bitcoin. Altcoins are created to address specific limitations or explore new use cases. Some prominent examples include:

- **Litecoin (LTC):** A faster, lighter version of Bitcoin with quicker transaction times and lower fees. Litecoin is often referred to as "silver to Bitcoin's gold."
- **Cardano (ADA):** Focused on scalability, sustainability, and academic research. Cardano's blockchain is designed to be highly secure and energy-efficient.
- **Solana (SOL):** Known for its high-speed, low-cost transactions. Solana's unique proof-of-stake consensus mechanism and parallel processing capabilities enable it to handle a large number of transactions per second.

Each altcoin brings unique features, often targeting niches like scalability, energy efficiency, or specific industries. For example, some altcoins are designed for privacy, while others focus on smart contract functionality or decentralized finance. By exploring the diverse landscape of altcoins, you can discover innovative solutions and potential investment opportunities.

4. Stablecoins: Bridging Crypto and Fiat

One common criticism of cryptocurrencies is their price volatility. Stablecoins solve this by pegging their value to a stable asset, like the US dollar or gold.

Why Stablecoins Are Important:

- **They enable low-risk transactions and are ideal for everyday payments.** Unlike volatile cryptocurrencies, stablecoins provide a more stable and predictable store of value.
- **Popular stablecoins like USDT (Tether) and USDC (USD Coin) are widely used in trading and decentralized finance.** These stablecoins facilitate smooth transactions and reduce the impact of market volatility.

Example Use Case: A freelancer in India can receive payment in USDC, bypassing the need for international bank transfers and currency conversion fees. This allows for faster, cheaper, and more efficient cross-border payments.

Stablecoins are essential for the growth of the cryptocurrency ecosystem, providing a bridge between the volatile world of cryptocurrencies and the stability of traditional fiat currencies.

5. Utility Tokens: Powering Ecosystems

Some cryptocurrencies, called utility tokens, are used to access or power specific platforms or services. For example:

- **Chainlink (LINK):** Connects smart contracts with real-world data, enabling them to interact with external systems like weather data, stock prices, and APIs. This allows for the creation of more complex and sophisticated dApps.
- **Vector Smart Gas (VSG):** Facilitates transactions and supports decentralized applications on the Vector Smart Chain. VSG serves as the native token of the Vector ecosystem, powering the platform and incentivizing user participation.

Utility tokens often play a critical role in incentivizing users and developers within their ecosystems. By providing access to specific services or granting voting rights, utility tokens can foster community engagement and drive the growth of the platform. As the blockchain ecosystem continues to evolve, utility tokens will likely play an increasingly important role in powering innovative and decentralized applications.

6. Governance Tokens: Shaping the Future

Governance tokens allow holders to vote on changes or improvements to a cryptocurrency's network or platform. This empowers communities to drive the evolution of projects.

Example: Uniswap's UNI Token lets holders vote on fee structures and future upgrades to the decentralized exchange.

By holding governance tokens, individuals can actively participate in shaping the future of their favorite crypto projects. This fosters a sense of ownership and community involvement, as token holders have a direct say in the decision-making process.

Governance tokens can be used to:

- **Vote on protocol upgrades:** Determine how the network evolves and adapts to changing market conditions.
- **Allocate treasury funds:** Decide how funds are spent on development, marketing, or other initiatives.
- **Propose and vote on new features:** Contribute to the innovation and growth of the project.

As the cryptocurrency ecosystem matures, governance tokens will play an increasingly important role in empowering communities and fostering decentralized decision-making.

7. Niche Coins: Specialized Use Cases

Some cryptocurrencies target very specific use cases or industries, such as:

- **Filecoin (FIL):** A decentralized file storage network that incentivizes users to store and share data. By leveraging blockchain technology, Filecoin aims to create a more secure, reliable, and affordable storage solution.
- **Axie Infinity (AXS):** An in-game currency for a blockchain-based game. Players can earn AXS tokens by playing the game, breeding digital creatures, and participating in battles.

- **Carbon Credit Tokens:** These tokens represent carbon offsets, which are credits for reducing carbon emissions. By tokenizing carbon credits, blockchain technology can help track and trade them more efficiently, promoting sustainability and environmental conservation.

These niche coins demonstrate how blockchain can be tailored for various industries. As technology continues to advance, we can expect to see even more innovative and specialized cryptocurrencies emerge.

8. Meme Coins: Community and Culture

Not all cryptocurrencies are created for technical reasons. Meme coins like Dogecoin (DOGE) and Shiba Inu (SHIB) started as jokes but gained massive followings thanks to online communities and social media.

Why They Matter:

- **They highlight the power of community in the crypto space.** Meme coins often have dedicated communities that actively promote and support the project, driving adoption and price appreciation.
- **Some, like Dogecoin, have evolved into legitimate payment options.** Dogecoin has been accepted by a growing number of merchants, demonstrating the potential of meme coins to become mainstream.

While meme coins often lack the technical innovation of other cryptocurrencies, they have a unique appeal that can drive significant price volatility and attract new investors to the crypto space. However, it's important to approach meme coin investments with caution, as their value can be highly speculative and subject to rapid fluctuations.

Why So Many Cryptocurrencies?

The proliferation of cryptocurrencies can be attributed to several factors:

- **Diverse Needs:** Each cryptocurrency is designed to address a unique problem or market. Some focus on decentralized finance, while others prioritize privacy, scalability, or specific industry applications. This diversity ensures that there's a cryptocurrency for every need.
- **Innovation:** The open-source nature of blockchain technology encourages experimentation and innovation. Developers around the world are constantly exploring new ideas and creating new cryptocurrencies to address specific challenges and opportunities.
- **Community-Driven Development:** Many cryptocurrencies are created by passionate communities that see a gap in the market. These communities contribute to the development, marketing, and adoption of their chosen cryptocurrency.

- **Speculation:** Some projects are launched to capitalize on market hype, often with unrealistic promises and unsustainable tokenomics. It's important to conduct thorough research and avoid investing in projects that lack a solid foundation or a clear use case.

While the sheer number of cryptocurrencies can be overwhelming, it also highlights the dynamism and innovation of the blockchain ecosystem. As the industry continues to evolve, we can expect to see new and exciting projects emerge, pushing the boundaries of what's possible with decentralized technology.

How to Navigate the Crypto Universe

With so many cryptocurrencies, how do you choose the right ones to explore or invest in? Here are some tips:

1. **Understand the Purpose:**

   - What problem does the cryptocurrency solve?
   - Does it offer a unique solution or a significant improvement over existing systems?
   - A clear and well-defined use case can indicate a strong project with potential for growth.

2. **Check the Team:**

   - Is the project backed by experienced and credible developers and advisors?

- A strong team with a proven track record can increase the project's chances of success.
- Look for team members with relevant expertise and a passion for the project.

3. **Review the Technology:**

    - Does the project offer real innovation or improvements over existing technologies?
    - Evaluate the technical soundness of the blockchain, the security of its protocols, and the scalability of its network.
    - Consider factors like transaction speed, fees, and energy efficiency.

4. **Look at the Community:**

    - A strong, active community often indicates a healthy and promising project.
    - Engage with the community on social media, forums, and other platforms to gauge their enthusiasm and support.
    - A passionate and supportive community can drive adoption and contribute to the project's long-term success.

By carefully considering these factors, you can make informed decisions and navigate the complex and dynamic world of cryptocurrencies. Remember to conduct thorough research, diversify your investments, and be prepared for market volatility.

WTF Does It All Mean?

The explosion of cryptocurrencies reflects the endless possibilities of blockchain technology. While Bitcoin started the revolution, thousands of other projects have emerged, each contributing to the ecosystem in unique ways.

Whether you're looking for a store of value, a tool for creating applications, or simply a fun meme coin, there's a cryptocurrency for you. However, it's important to approach the crypto world with caution and a clear understanding of the risks involved.

As the cryptocurrency landscape continues to evolve, it's crucial to stay informed, conduct thorough research, and make informed decisions. By embracing the potential of blockchain technology and understanding the risks, you can navigate this exciting and dynamic space with confidence.

Chapter 1.4:

Key Terminology What You Need to Know

The world of cryptocurrency is full of new and often confusing terms. Understanding the key terminology is crucial for navigating this space with confidence. Here's a beginner-friendly glossary of the most important terms you need to know.

As you delve deeper into the world of cryptocurrency, you'll encounter a variety of concepts and technologies. From the underlying blockchain technology to the various applications built on it, it's essential to have a solid grasp of the key terms. This glossary will help you understand the basics and equip you with the knowledge needed to make informed decisions.

By familiarizing yourself with these terms, you'll be able to confidently discuss cryptocurrency topics, evaluate investment opportunities, and participate in the growing crypto community. Whether you're a seasoned investor or a curious newcomer, this glossary will serve as a valuable resource on your journey into the exciting world of cryptocurrency.

1. Blockchain

The underlying technology behind cryptocurrencies, a blockchain is a decentralized digital ledger that records transactions in a secure, transparent, and tamper-proof way. Think of it as a digital notebook where every transaction is written in permanent ink, and copies are shared across thousands of computers.

How Does it Work?

Each transaction on the blockchain is grouped into blocks. Once a block is filled with transactions, it's added to the chain, creating a permanent and unchangeable record. This process is called mining, and it involves powerful computers solving complex mathematical problems.

Why is it Important?

Blockchains offer a secure and efficient way to track and verify transactions without the need for intermediaries like banks. This makes them ideal for a wide range of applications, from finance to supply chain management. Additionally, the decentralized nature of blockchains makes them resistant to censorship and fraud.

Think of it as: A digital notebook where every transaction is written in permanent ink, and copies are shared across thousands of computers.

2. Cryptocurrency

A digital or virtual currency that uses cryptography for security and operates on blockchain technology. Examples include Bitcoin (BTC), Ethereum (ETH), and Vector Smart Gas (VSG). Cryptocurrencies are decentralized, meaning they aren't controlled by any government or institution.

How Does it Work?

Cryptocurrencies use blockchain technology to record transactions. Each transaction is verified by a network of computers, ensuring security and transparency. To use cryptocurrency, you need a digital wallet to store your coins. You can then use your wallet to send and receive cryptocurrency.

Why is it Important?

Cryptocurrencies offer a new way to transact and store value. They can be used for various purposes, from sending money to buying goods and services. Additionally, cryptocurrencies can provide financial inclusion to people who are unbanked or underbanked.

Key Point: Cryptocurrencies are decentralized, meaning they aren't controlled by any government or institution.

3. Wallet

A digital tool used to store, send, and receive cryptocurrencies. There are two main types:

- **Hot Wallets:** Connected to the internet (e.g., mobile or desktop wallets).
- **Cold Wallets:** Offline and more secure (e.g., hardware wallets like Ledger or Trezor).

How Does it Work?

Wallets store your public and private keys. Your public key is like your email address, anyone can see it and send you cryptocurrency. Your private key is like your password, only you should know it, and it's used to access and spend your cryptocurrency.

Why is it Important?

Wallets are essential for anyone who wants to participate in the cryptocurrency ecosystem. They provide a safe and convenient way to manage your crypto assets. By understanding the difference between hot and cold wallets, you can choose the best option for your security needs.

Pro Tip: Always back up your wallet and keep your private key secure. A private key is like a password to your cryptocurrency, so it's crucial to protect it.

4. Private Key

A unique string of characters that acts as a password to access your cryptocurrency. Whoever holds the private key controls the funds.

How Does It Work?

When you create a cryptocurrency wallet, a pair of keys is generated: a public key and a private key. The public key is used to receive cryptocurrency, while the private key is used to sign transactions and prove ownership of the funds.

Why is it Important?

Your private key is the key to your cryptocurrency kingdom. It's crucial to protect it, as it gives you sole control over your digital assets. However, this power comes with great responsibility. If you lose your private key, there's no way to recover it, and your funds will be lost forever.

Important: Never share your private key. If it's lost or stolen, your funds are gone forever.

5. Public Key

A cryptographic code linked to your private key that you can share with others to receive cryptocurrency. Think of it as your email address. People can send you funds without accessing your private key.

How Does It Work?

When you create a cryptocurrency wallet, a pair of keys is generated: a public key and a private key. The public key is used to receive cryptocurrency, while the private key is used to sign transactions and prove ownership of the funds. You can share your public key with anyone, but your private key should remain secret.

Why is it Important?

Public keys allow for secure and efficient transactions on the blockchain. By sharing your public key, you can receive payments from anyone, anywhere in the world.

6. Token vs. Coin

- **Coin:** A cryptocurrency that operates on its own blockchain (e.g., Bitcoin, Ethereum).
- **Token:** A digital asset built on another blockchain (e.g., ERC-20 tokens on Ethereum).

Why is the Distinction Important? Understanding the difference between coins and tokens is crucial for navigating the complex world of cryptocurrencies. Coins have their own blockchains and typically offer more flexibility and control. Tokens, on the other hand, rely on the security and infrastructure of the blockchain they are built on.

Example: VSG is a coin because it will operate on its own blockchain, the Vector Smart Chain.

7. Mining

The process of validating transactions and adding them to the blockchain by solving complex mathematical puzzles. Miners are rewarded with cryptocurrency.

How Does It Work?

Miners use powerful computers to solve complex mathematical problems. The first miner to solve a problem adds a new block of transactions to the blockchain and is rewarded with cryptocurrency. This process helps to secure the blockchain and incentivizes miners to participate in the network.

Used In: Proof-of-Work (PoW) systems like Bitcoin.

Why is it Important?

Mining is essential for maintaining the security and integrity of blockchains. It ensures that transactions are verified and added to the blockchain in a transparent and tamper-proof manner.

8. Staking

Locking up your cryptocurrency to help validate transactions and secure the network. In return, you earn rewards.

How Does It Work?

In a proof-of-stake system, instead of miners competing to solve complex puzzles, validators are selected to validate transactions based on the amount of cryptocurrency they stake. The more cryptocurrency you stake, the higher your chances of being selected to validate transactions and earn rewards.

Used In: Proof-of-Stake (PoS) systems like Ethereum 2.0.

Why is it Important?

Staking is a more energy-efficient and environmentally friendly way to secure blockchains. It also encourages long-term holding of cryptocurrency and fosters a more decentralized network.

9. Gas Fees

Gas fees are the transaction fees paid to miners or validators to process a transaction on a blockchain.

How Do They Work?

Gas fees are typically denominated in the native cryptocurrency of the blockchain. The amount of gas fee required for a transaction depends on factors such as the complexity of the transaction, network congestion, and the current price of gas.

Example: On Ethereum, you pay gas fees to execute smart contracts or send tokens.

Why Are They Important?

Gas fees help to incentivize miners or validators to process transactions efficiently and securely. They also help to manage network congestion by discouraging frivolous or low-value transactions. However, high gas fees can sometimes deter users from interacting with certain blockchains, especially during periods of high demand.

10. Smart Contract

Self-executing agreements where the terms are written directly into code. Once conditions are met, the contract automatically executes.

How Do They Work?

Smart contracts are deployed on blockchains and can be triggered by specific events or conditions. For instance, a smart contract could automatically release funds to a vendor once a shipment is confirmed or a service is delivered.

Example: A smart contract could release payment to a freelancer once the job is marked complete.

Why Are They Important?

Smart contracts offer a new way to automate and enforce agreements without the need for intermediaries. They can increase transparency, reduce costs, and improve efficiency in a wide range of industries.

11. Decentralized Finance (DeFi)

Financial services built on blockchain technology that don't rely on traditional intermediaries like banks. Popular DeFi activities include lending, borrowing, and trading. Think of it as banking without the banks.

How Does It Work?

DeFi applications leverage smart contracts to automate financial processes, making them more accessible and transparent. For example, you can lend cryptocurrency to others and earn interest without needing a traditional bank. Similarly, you can borrow cryptocurrency using your own cryptocurrency as collateral.

Why is it Important?

DeFi offers a new way to access financial services, particularly for those who are unbanked or underbanked. By removing intermediaries, DeFi can reduce costs and increase financial inclusion. However, it's important to be aware of the risks associated with DeFi, such as smart contract vulnerabilities and market volatility.

12. Decentralized Applications (dApps)

Applications that run on a blockchain instead of centralized servers. They're often open-source and provide various services like trading, gaming, or social networking.

How Do They Work?

dApps leverage the power of blockchain technology to create decentralized, transparent, and censorship-resistant applications. They interact with smart contracts to execute transactions and enforce rules, eliminating the need for intermediaries.

Example: Uniswap is a dApp for decentralized trading.

Why Are They Important?

dApps have the potential to revolutionize various industries by offering more transparency, security, and user control. They can empower individuals and communities to build and participate in decentralized ecosystems, fostering innovation and economic opportunity.

13. Stablecoin

A type of cryptocurrency pegged to a stable asset, such as the US dollar or gold, to reduce volatility.

How Do They Work?

Stablecoins aim to maintain a stable value by backing each coin with a corresponding amount of the underlying asset. This helps to mitigate the price fluctuations often associated with other cryptocurrencies.

Popular Examples: USDT (Tether), USDC (USD Coin).

Why Are They Important?

Stablecoins provide a more stable store of value and a medium of exchange compared to volatile cryptocurrencies. They can be useful for various purposes, such as making payments, trading, and hedging against market volatility.

14. NFT (Non-Fungible Token)

A unique digital asset that represents ownership of a specific item, such as art, music, or collectibles. Unlike cryptocurrencies, NFTs cannot be exchanged on a one-to-one basis.

How Do They Work?

NFTs are created on blockchains and use smart contracts to verify ownership and authenticity. Each NFT has a unique identifier, making it distinct from other NFTs.

Example: Digital artwork sold as an NFT on OpenSea.

Why Are They Important?

NFTs have opened up new possibilities for digital ownership and creators. They allow artists and creators to monetize their work directly, without intermediaries. Additionally, NFTs can be used to represent real-world assets, such as real estate or luxury goods, on the blockchain.

15. Rug Pull

A type of scam where developers abandon a project and run off with investors' funds.

How to Avoid:

- **Research projects carefully:** Look into the team behind the project, their experience, and their track record.
- **Look for audits:** Reputable projects often undergo security audits to identify and address potential vulnerabilities.
- **Avoid investments that seem too good to be true:** High returns with low risk are often signs of a scam.
- **Diversify your investments:** Don't put all your eggs in one basket. Spread your investments across multiple projects.

By following these tips, you can help protect yourself from rug pulls and other scams in the cryptocurrency space.

16. Whale

An individual or entity that holds a large amount of cryptocurrency, often capable of influencing market prices with their trades.

Why Are Whales Important?

Whales can significantly impact the price of a cryptocurrency, especially in less liquid markets. Their large-scale buying or selling activities can cause sudden price swings, making it important for traders to be aware of their movements.

Example: A Bitcoin whale might hold tens of thousands of BTC.

Understanding the role of whales can help investors make informed decisions and navigate the volatile cryptocurrency market.

17. FOMO (Fear of Missing Out)

The anxiety of missing a lucrative investment opportunity, often leading to impulsive buying.

Why is it Dangerous?

FOMO can lead to irrational decision-making and poor investment choices. It can cause you to invest in projects without proper research or risk assessment, increasing your chances of financial loss.

Tip: Stick to your strategy and avoid emotional decisions.

To combat **FOMO**, it's essential to have a well-defined investment strategy and stick to it. Conduct thorough research, diversify your portfolio, and set realistic expectations. Remember, patience and discipline are key to successful investing.

18. HODL

A popular term in the crypto community that means "Hold On for Dear Life." It encourages long-term holding of cryptocurrencies rather than selling during market fluctuations.

Why is it Important?

The **HODL** strategy can be beneficial for long-term investors who believe in the underlying technology and potential of cryptocurrencies. By holding onto their investments during market downturns, HODLers can potentially benefit from significant price increases in the future.

Fun Fact: The term originated from a misspelled forum post in 2013.

It's important to note that the **HODL** strategy is not without risk. Market conditions can change rapidly, and it's essential to conduct thorough research and consider your risk tolerance before making any investment decisions.

19. ICO/IDO (Initial Coin Offering/Initial DEX Offering)

Ways for crypto projects to raise funds by selling tokens to investors.

- **ICO**: Tokens are sold directly from the project team.
- **IDO**: Tokens are launched on a decentralized exchange.

Example: VSG's launch through an IEO (Initial Exchange Offering).

Why Are They Important?

ICOs and IDOs provide a way for crypto projects to raise capital and fund development. They also offer investors an opportunity to participate in the early stages of promising projects. However, it's important to exercise caution when investing in ICOs and IDOs, as there is a high risk of fraud and scams.

20. Blockchain Explorer

A tool that allows you to view blockchain transactions in real time. You can search by wallet address, transaction ID, or block number.

How Does It Work?

Blockchain explorers index and store information about transactions and blocks on a blockchain. This allows users to track the movement of funds, verify transaction details, and gain insights into the network's activity.

Example: EtherScan for Ethereum or VSC's own block explorer.

Why Are They Important?

Blockchain explorers provide transparency and accountability in the cryptocurrency ecosystem. They allow users to verify the authenticity of transactions, track the progress of projects, and gain a deeper understanding of how blockchains function.

WTF Does It All Mean?

Learning the language of cryptocurrency is the first step to understanding this new financial and technological ecosystem.

Don't worry if it feels overwhelming at first—these terms will become second nature as you engage more with the crypto world.

By familiarizing yourself with the key terms and concepts, you'll be able to:

- **Make informed decisions:** Understand the risks and rewards associated with different cryptocurrencies and blockchain projects.
- **Engage with the community:** Participate in discussions, forums, and social media groups to learn from others and share your knowledge.
- **Stay up-to-date with the latest trends:** Keep track of the latest developments in the crypto space, including new projects, technological advancements, and regulatory changes.

Pro Tip: Bookmark this glossary as a quick reference guide. The more you familiarize yourself with these terms, the more confident you'll feel on your crypto journey.

Remember, the crypto world is constantly evolving, so it's important to stay curious and keep learning. By embracing this mindset, you can unlock the full potential of this exciting and innovative technology.

Chapter 1.5:

Why Cryptocurrency Matters

Cryptocurrency is more than just a trend or investment opportunity—it's a transformative technology that is reshaping finance, technology, and the global economy. This section explores why cryptocurrency is important, its key benefits, and its potential to change the way we interact with money and systems.

Key Benefits of Cryptocurrency:

- **Decentralization:** Cryptocurrencies operate on decentralized networks, eliminating the need for intermediaries like banks or governments. This makes them more resistant to censorship, fraud, and systemic failures.
- **Security:** Blockchain technology ensures the security of transactions through cryptographic techniques, making it difficult for hackers to manipulate or compromise the system.

- **Transparency:** All transactions on the blockchain are public and transparent, increasing accountability and reducing the risk of fraudulent activities.
- **Accessibility:** Cryptocurrencies can provide financial inclusion to billions of people who are unbanked or underbanked, giving them access to financial services that were previously out of reach.
- **Innovation:** Cryptocurrencies are driving innovation in various sectors, from finance to supply chain management and healthcare. By leveraging blockchain technology, businesses can streamline operations, reduce costs, and improve efficiency.

The Future of Finance:

Cryptocurrency has the potential to revolutionize the way we think about money and finance. By offering a decentralized, secure, and transparent alternative to traditional financial systems, cryptocurrencies can empower individuals and businesses alike.

As the technology continues to evolve, we can expect to see even more innovative applications of cryptocurrency, from decentralized finance (DeFi) to non-fungible tokens (NFTs).

By understanding the fundamental principles of cryptocurrency and blockchain technology, you can position yourself to take advantage of the opportunities that lie ahead.

1. Empowering Individuals: Financial Freedom

Traditional financial systems rely on centralized institutions like banks and governments. These systems:

- **Can exclude people without access to traditional banking.** Many people, particularly in developing countries, are unable to open bank accounts or access financial services.
- **Charge high fees for services like international money transfers.** These fees can make it difficult for individuals and businesses to send and receive money across borders.
- **Are vulnerable to inflation, economic instability, and corruption.** Central banks can manipulate the money supply, leading to inflation and devaluation of currency. Additionally, corruption and mismanagement can erode trust in traditional financial systems.

Cryptocurrency: A New Paradigm

Cryptocurrency gives power back to individuals.

- **You don't need a bank to store or transfer funds—just a crypto wallet and internet access.** This empowers individuals to take control of their finances and make their own decisions.
- **No one can freeze your account or impose arbitrary restrictions.** Cryptocurrencies offer a more secure and private way to manage your assets.

- **Transactions are borderless, instant, and cost-effective.** This enables faster and cheaper international transfers, particularly for people living in countries with weak financial infrastructure.

Real-World Example: In countries with hyperinflation, like Venezuela, people are turning to Bitcoin to preserve their wealth and access global markets. By using cryptocurrency, they can bypass the limitations of their local currency and protect their savings from economic instability.

Cryptocurrency offers a promising alternative to traditional finance, empowering individuals and challenging the status quo.

2. Increasing Global Accessibility

There are billions of unbanked or underbanked people worldwide who lack access to financial services. Cryptocurrency provides an alternative:

- **Anyone with an internet connection can use it.** This makes cryptocurrency accessible to people in remote areas or countries with limited banking infrastructure.
- **It enables financial inclusion for marginalized communities.** By removing the barriers to entry associated with traditional banking, cryptocurrency can empower individuals and businesses to participate in the global economy.

Why It Matters:

- **Entrepreneurs in developing countries can access global markets without intermediaries.** This can help stimulate economic growth and create jobs.
- **Workers abroad can send remittances home without losing a significant portion to fees.** Cryptocurrency-based remittance services can be faster, cheaper, and more secure than traditional methods.

Example: Stablecoins like USDC are being used in parts of Africa to enable cross-border trade and payments where traditional banking infrastructure is lacking. By providing a stable and reliable medium of exchange, stablecoins can help to boost economic activity and improve the lives of millions of people.

Cryptocurrency has the potential to revolutionize the global financial system, making it more inclusive, efficient, and equitable.

3. Transparency and Trust: A Trustless System

Trust in traditional systems is often broken by scandals, fraud, or mismanagement. Cryptocurrencies operate on transparent blockchains where every transaction is publicly recorded.

Why It Matters:

- **Reduces corruption by ensuring accountability.** The transparency of blockchain technology makes it difficult

for individuals or organizations to engage in fraudulent activities.
- **Enables trustless interactions, where participants don't need to know or trust each other for transactions to work.** Smart contracts automate the execution of agreements, reducing the need for intermediaries and minimizing the risk of disputes.

Example: Ethereum's blockchain supports decentralized finance (DeFi) protocols, where smart contracts replace banks as the trusted intermediary. This allows users to lend, borrow, and trade cryptocurrencies directly with each other, without the need for traditional financial institutions.

By fostering trust and transparency, blockchain technology can revolutionize various industries, from finance to supply chain management and healthcare.

4. Efficiency and Cost Reduction

Traditional financial systems are often slow and expensive, especially for cross-border transactions. Banks rely on intermediaries and outdated systems that add delays and fees. Cryptocurrency simplifies this process.

- **Transactions are processed directly between users, cutting out intermediaries.** This eliminates the need for banks and other financial institutions to facilitate transactions, reducing costs and increasing efficiency.

- **Payments can be settled in minutes, not days.** This allows for faster and more convenient transactions, particularly for businesses that need to make quick payments or receive funds from international clients.

Real-World Impact:

- **Sending Bitcoin internationally costs a fraction of what banks or remittance services charge.** This can save individuals and businesses significant amounts of money, particularly for cross-border transactions.
- **Businesses can reduce costs by using blockchain for supply chain management.** By tracking the movement of goods on a blockchain, businesses can improve transparency, reduce fraud, and streamline their operations.

By streamlining processes and reducing costs, cryptocurrency can help to drive economic growth and improve the efficiency of global commerce.

5. Innovation and New Opportunities

Cryptocurrency is driving innovation in areas like:

- **Decentralized Finance (DeFi):** DeFi platforms allow individuals to access financial services, such as lending, borrowing, and trading, without the need for traditional financial institutions. This empowers individuals and creates new opportunities for financial inclusion.

- **NFTs (Non-Fungible Tokens):** NFTs represent unique digital assets, such as art, music, or collectibles. They enable artists and creators to tokenize their work, sell it directly to collectors, and receive royalties on secondary sales.
- **DAOs (Decentralized Autonomous Organizations):** DAOs are autonomous organizations governed by rules encoded as computer programs known as smart contracts. This allows for transparent, efficient, and community-driven decision-making.

Example: Projects like Uniswap allow users to trade cryptocurrencies directly with each other without relying on centralized exchanges. This peer-to-peer trading platform eliminates the need for intermediaries, reducing fees and increasing transparency.

By fostering innovation and disrupting traditional industries, cryptocurrency is shaping the future of finance, technology, and society as a whole.

6. Protecting Against Inflation

Inflation erodes the purchasing power of traditional currencies. Many cryptocurrencies, like Bitcoin, have a fixed supply or predictable issuance rates, making them an attractive store of value.

Why It Matters:

- **Cryptocurrencies act as a hedge against inflation in unstable economies.** By limiting the supply of tokens, cryptocurrencies can maintain their value over time, even as traditional currencies lose purchasing power.
- **Investors see Bitcoin as "digital gold" due to its scarcity.** Just like gold, Bitcoin's limited supply makes it a desirable asset for investors seeking to protect their wealth.

Example: During periods of economic instability, Bitcoin's value has surged as people seek alternatives to fiat currency. This highlights the potential of cryptocurrency as a hedge against inflation and a store of value.

By understanding the impact of inflation and the role of cryptocurrency as a potential hedge, investors can make informed decisions about their financial future.

7. Decentralization: Reducing Single Points of Failure

Centralized systems are prone to failures, hacks, and censorship. Blockchain's decentralized nature distributes control across a network of nodes, reducing these risks.

Why It Matters:

- **No single entity can manipulate the system or shut it down.** This makes blockchain networks more resilient to attacks and censorship.

- **Decentralization enhances security and reliability.** By distributing data and processing power across multiple nodes, blockchain systems are less vulnerable to single points of failure.

Example: The Ethereum blockchain continued to operate seamlessly even during major global events, thanks to its decentralized infrastructure. This resilience demonstrates the strength of decentralized systems in the face of adversity.

By decentralizing power and control, blockchain technology promotes a more equitable and democratic digital future.

8. Shaping the Future

Cryptocurrency isn't just changing money—it's changing how we think about ownership, collaboration, and innovation. Some potential future impacts include:

- **Tokenized Assets:** Real-world assets like real estate, art, or stocks can be represented as digital tokens on the blockchain. This can make it easier to buy, sell, and trade fractional ownership of these assets, increasing liquidity and accessibility.
- **Digital Identity:** Blockchain technology can be used to create secure, decentralized digital identities. This can help to reduce identity theft and fraud, and streamline processes like passport verification and online authentication.

- **Sustainability:** Blockchain can be used to track and verify carbon credits or renewable energy certificates, promoting transparency and accountability in the sustainability sector.

As blockchain technology continues to evolve, we can expect to see even more innovative applications emerge, transforming various industries and reshaping the future of our society.

Challenges to Overcome

While cryptocurrency has enormous potential, it's not without challenges:

- **Volatility:** The prices of cryptocurrencies can fluctuate wildly, making it difficult to use them as a stable medium of exchange. However, as the market matures and becomes more stable, volatility may decrease.
- **Regulation:** Governments around the world are still grappling with how to regulate the cryptocurrency industry. Regulatory uncertainty can create challenges for businesses and individuals operating in this space.
- **Adoption:** Mass adoption of cryptocurrency requires user-friendly tools and widespread education. As the technology continues to evolve and become more accessible, adoption rates are expected to increase.

These challenges represent opportunities for innovation and growth. By addressing these issues, the cryptocurrency industry can continue to mature and realize its full potential. As the technology evolves and becomes more mainstream, we can expect to see increased stability, regulatory clarity, and widespread adoption.

WTF Does It All Mean?

Cryptocurrency matters because it represents a shift in power from centralized institutions to individuals. It's not just about digital money—it's about creating a fairer, more accessible, and more efficient system for everyone.

By understanding the fundamental principles of cryptocurrency and blockchain technology, you can unlock a world of possibilities. You can participate in the decentralized economy, explore innovative applications, and contribute to the future of finance and technology.

Whether you're here to invest, build, or simply learn, understanding why cryptocurrency matters is the first step to appreciating its transformative potential. By embracing this technology and its underlying principles, you can empower yourself and help shape the future of the digital world.

Chapter 1.6:

Bringing It Home

As we conclude this foundational part of your crypto journey, let's take a moment to reflect on what you've learned so far and why it's important. You've explored the evolution of money, the basics of blockchain technology, and the unique value cryptocurrency brings to the table. By now, you should have a clearer understanding of what makes crypto a revolutionary force—and why it matters to you.

Remember, the world of cryptocurrency is constantly evolving. Stay curious, keep learning, and most importantly, stay safe. By understanding the fundamentals and staying informed, you can navigate this exciting and dynamic space with confidence.

The future of finance and technology is being shaped by blockchain and cryptocurrency. As you continue your journey, you'll have the opportunity to be part of this revolution and contribute to shaping a more decentralized, transparent, and equitable future.

Why This Knowledge Matters

Understanding cryptocurrency is more than just keeping up with a trend; it's about equipping yourself for a rapidly evolving future. Here's why this knowledge is essential:

- **Empowerment:** Cryptocurrency gives you control over your money, your assets, and your financial future. By understanding the principles of blockchain technology and the benefits of decentralized finance, you can take control of your financial destiny.
- **Opportunities:** The crypto space is full of exciting opportunities for innovation and growth. From investing in promising projects to building your own decentralized applications, the possibilities are endless.
- **Preparedness:** As crypto adoption grows, being knowledgeable about the technology and its implications will help you make informed decisions and avoid potential pitfalls. By understanding the risks and rewards, you can navigate the crypto landscape with confidence.

By acquiring a solid understanding of cryptocurrency, you can position yourself to benefit from the transformative potential of this technology. Whether you're an investor, a developer, or simply someone curious about the future of finance, this knowledge will serve you well.

Your Journey Starts Here

Entering the world of cryptocurrency might feel overwhelming, but remember: every expert was once a beginner. The key is to take one step at a time:

- **Start by setting up a wallet:** A cryptocurrency wallet is a digital tool that allows you to store, send, and receive cryptocurrencies. We'll guide you through the process of choosing and setting up a secure wallet in the next chapter.
- **Learn the basics of buying and storing cryptocurrency safely:** Understand the different ways to purchase cryptocurrency, from exchanges to decentralized platforms. We'll also cover best practices for securing your wallet and protecting your assets.
- **Explore the growing ecosystem of applications and opportunities:** Discover the exciting world of decentralized finance (DeFi), non-fungible tokens (NFTs), and other innovative applications built on blockchain technology.

By the end of this book, you'll have the tools and confidence to navigate the crypto world like a pro. Remember, the journey of a thousand miles begins with a single step. So let's take that first step together and embark on an exciting adventure into the future of finance and technology.

Looking Ahead

The next chapter is where things get hands-on. We'll guide you step-by-step through setting up your first cryptocurrency wallet—a crucial tool for managing your digital assets. From there, you'll learn how to buy your first cryptocurrency, build a portfolio, and stay safe in the process.

Whether you're here to invest, use crypto in your daily life, or simply understand the technology, this journey will empower you to make the most of this exciting new frontier.

Remember, the crypto space is constantly evolving, so it's important to stay updated on the latest trends and developments. By following the guidance in this book and staying curious, you can position yourself to take advantage of the opportunities that lie ahead.

Final Thoughts

The crypto revolution is here, and you're now a part of it. By taking the time to learn and explore, you're positioning yourself at the forefront of a transformative movement. The knowledge you gain today will not only help you navigate the present but also prepare you for the future.

As you embark on your crypto journey, remember to embrace the learning process and be patient with yourself. The crypto space can be complex, but with the right information and guidance, you can successfully navigate its challenges and opportunities.

Let's take the next step together. Your first crypto wallet—and your first step into the world of blockchain—is just a chapter away.

By the time you finish this book, you'll be well-equipped to harness the power of cryptocurrency and shape your own financial future.

Chapter 2:

Getting Started with Wallets

What is a Crypto Wallet, and Why Do You Need One?

In the world of cryptocurrency, your wallet is your gateway to storing, sending, and receiving digital assets. Unlike traditional wallets that hold physical cash, crypto wallets store keys—the cryptographic codes that give you access to your digital funds.

There are two types of keys associated with every wallet:

- **Public Key:** Similar to a bank account number, it's a string of characters that you can share with others so they can send you cryptocurrency.
- **Private Key:** Your secret password, it grants you sole access to your funds. It's crucial to keep your private key secure, as anyone who has access to it can control your wallet.

Why You Need a Wallet:

- It's the tool that lets you interact with the blockchain.

- Without a wallet, you can't store, send, or receive cryptocurrencies.

Think of your crypto wallet as a digital safe that holds your valuable assets. By understanding the importance of wallets and how to use them securely, you can confidently navigate the world of cryptocurrency.

Types of Crypto Wallets

Choosing the right wallet depends on your needs, whether you prioritize convenience, security, or accessibility. Let's explore the two main types of wallets:

1. Hot Wallets:

- Connected to the internet.
- Ideal for frequent transactions.
- **Examples:** Mobile wallets, desktop wallets, browser extensions.

Pros: Easy to set up and use.

Cons: Vulnerable to hacking if not secured properly.

Popular Hot Wallets:

- **MetaMask:** A popular browser extension that supports Ethereum and other compatible blockchains. It's easy to use and integrates seamlessly with various decentralized applications.

- **Phantom:** A user-friendly Solana wallet that offers a seamless experience for interacting with the Solana ecosystem.
- **Trust Wallet:** A versatile wallet that supports multiple blockchains, including Ethereum and Binance Smart Chain. It offers a range of features, such as staking and decentralized exchange access.

2. Cold Wallets:

- Offline wallets that are disconnected from the internet.
- Ideal for long-term storage and security.
- **Examples:** Hardware wallets, paper wallets.

Pros: Highly secure and immune to online hacking.

Cons: Less convenient for frequent use.

Popular Cold Wallets:

- **Ledger Nano X:** A popular hardware wallet that supports a wide range of cryptocurrencies and offers advanced security features.
- **Trezor:** Another popular hardware wallet known for its robust security and ease of use.

By understanding the pros and cons of different wallet types, you can choose the best option to meet your specific needs and security requirements.

Step-by-Step Guide: Setting Up Your First Wallet

Let's walk through setting up a wallet, using MetaMask as an example. MetaMask is a free and easy-to-use browser extension wallet for Ethereum and other blockchains compatible with the Ethereum Virtual Machine (EVM).

Download and Install MetaMask:

1. Visit the official website (metamask.io) and download the extension for your browser. Make sure you're on the official website to avoid downloading malware disguised as MetaMask.

2. Choose your browser from the list (Chrome, Firefox, Brave, etc.) and follow the installation instructions. The process is similar across most browsers and typically involves adding the extension from the official web store.

Additional Notes:

MetaMask also allows you to connect to decentralized applications (dApps) built on the Ethereum blockchain. This lets you interact with DeFi platforms, NFT marketplaces, and other innovative applications within the crypto ecosystem.

Create a New Wallet:

1. Once the extension is installed, open MetaMask and click on "Create a Wallet."

2. Choose a strong password. This password will be used to access your wallet on this specific device. Don't reuse passwords you use for other online accounts.

3. Secure Your Seed Phrase: This is the most crucial step. MetaMask will generate a 12-word seed phrase, also known as a recovery phrase or mnemonic seed. This phrase acts as a master key to your wallet and allows you to recover your funds on any device if you lose access to your current device.

    o **Write down the seed phrase on a piece of paper.** Do not store it digitally or share it with anyone! Treat it with the same importance as you would your bank account information.
    o Consider using a metal seed phrase recovery kit for added security. These kits are fire and water-resistant and provide a more durable way to store your seed phrase.

4. Verify your seed phrase by re-entering the words in the correct order.

5. Congratulations! You've now created your first crypto wallet.

Additional Notes:

Remember, it's important to be cautious when using your wallet. Never share your seed phrase or password with anyone, and be wary of phishing scams that try to trick you into revealing your private information.

Start Using Your Wallet:

1. You'll see your public address, which looks like a long string of alphanumeric characters. This address is similar to your bank account number and can be shared with others to receive cryptocurrency.

2. To send or receive cryptocurrency, you'll need to add funds to your wallet. This can be done in a few ways:

    - **Transfer cryptocurrency from an exchange:** Purchase cryptocurrency on a crypto exchange like Coinbase or Binance and then transfer it to your MetaMask wallet address.
    - **Receive cryptocurrency from another wallet:** Someone else can send cryptocurrency directly to your MetaMask public address.

By following these steps and taking security precautions seriously, you can safely set up your first crypto wallet and begin exploring the exciting world of cryptocurrency.

Best Practices for Wallet Security

To ensure the security of your cryptocurrency, it's crucial to follow best practices:

Never Share Your Private Key or Seed Phrase:

- Treat it like your bank PIN—keep it private and secure.
- Avoid writing it down on easily accessible paper or storing it digitally.

Enable Two-Factor Authentication (2FA):

- If your wallet supports it, enable 2FA for added security. This adds an extra layer of protection by requiring a second verification step, such as a code sent to your phone.

Avoid Public Wi-Fi:

- When accessing your wallet, use a secure internet connection. Public Wi-Fi networks are often vulnerable to hacking attempts.

Back Up Your Wallet:

- Store multiple copies of your seed phrase in safe locations (e.g., a safe deposit box, a fireproof safe, or a secure digital storage device).
- Consider using a password manager to securely store your seed phrase.

Use Hardware Wallets for Large Amounts:

- For significant cryptocurrency holdings, consider using a hardware wallet like Ledger or Trezor.

- These devices store your private keys offline, making them highly secure.

By following these best practices, you can significantly reduce the risk of unauthorized access to your funds and protect your investments. Remember, security is paramount in the world of cryptocurrency.

How to Choose the Right Wallet for You

When selecting a cryptocurrency wallet, consider the following factors:

Security:

- **Cold Wallets:** Offer the highest level of security by storing your private keys offline. They are ideal for long-term storage of large amounts of cryptocurrency.
- **Hot Wallets:** While convenient for frequent transactions, they are more susceptible to hacking attacks. Use strong passwords, enable two-factor authentication, and be cautious about phishing attempts.

Ease of Use:

- **User Interface:** Look for a wallet with a user-friendly interface that is easy to navigate.
- **Mobile Compatibility:** If you prefer to manage your crypto on the go, choose a wallet with a mobile app.

Supported Cryptocurrencies:

- Ensure the wallet supports the specific cryptocurrencies you want to use. Some wallets are designed for specific blockchains, while others offer broader compatibility.

Additional Features:

- Consider features like staking, decentralized exchange integration, and NFT support.

Popular Wallet Options

- Hardware Wallets:
    - **Ledger Nano X:** A popular hardware wallet offering advanced security features and support for multiple blockchains.
    - **Trezor Model T:** Another reliable hardware wallet known for its robust security and user-friendly interface.

- Software Wallets:
    - **MetaMask:** A browser extension and mobile app that supports Ethereum and other EVM-compatible blockchains.
    - **Trust Wallet:** A mobile wallet that supports a wide range of blockchains and offers features like staking and decentralized exchange access.

- - **Coinbase Wallet:** A non-custodial wallet that allows you to store, send, and receive various cryptocurrencies.

- **Mobile Wallets:**

  - **Exodus:** A user-friendly mobile wallet that supports multiple cryptocurrencies and offers features like staking and swapping.
  - **Coinbase Wallet:** The mobile version of the Coinbase Wallet, offering similar features to the browser extension.

Ultimately, the best wallet for you will depend on your specific needs and preferences. By considering the factors mentioned above, you can choose a wallet that offers the right balance of security, convenience, and functionality.

Tips for Beginners

As you embark on your cryptocurrency journey, here are a few tips to help you get started:

1. **Start Small:** When setting up your first wallet, practice by transferring a small amount of cryptocurrency to get comfortable with the process. This will help you understand the mechanics of sending and receiving funds without risking significant amounts of money.
2. **Test the Waters:** Send and receive small transactions to gain experience and build confidence. This will help you

familiarize yourself with the wallet interface and the process of interacting with the blockchain.

3. **Explore Multi-Chain Wallets:** Consider using a multi-chain wallet like Trust Wallet or SafePal, which supports multiple blockchains. This allows you to manage various cryptocurrencies from a single platform, simplifying your portfolio management.

4. **Stay Informed:** Keep up-to-date with the latest news and developments in the cryptocurrency space. Follow reputable news sources, join online communities, and learn from experienced users.

5. **Prioritize Security:** Always prioritize the security of your wallet and private keys. Use strong passwords, enable two-factor authentication, and be cautious of phishing attempts.

By following these tips and taking a gradual approach, you can safely and confidently navigate the world of cryptocurrency. Remember, the most important thing is to start learning and experimenting. With time and practice, you'll become more comfortable and proficient in managing your digital assets.

WTF Does It All Mean?

Your wallet is your key to the world of cryptocurrency. By setting one up, you're taking the first tangible step into this exciting ecosystem. Whether you choose a hot wallet for daily use or a cold wallet for long-term storage, make security your top priority.

In the next chapter, we'll guide you through buying your first cryptocurrency, so you can start filling that shiny new wallet with digital assets. We'll explore different buying methods, from centralized exchanges to decentralized platforms, and discuss the importance of choosing reputable and secure platforms.

Pro Tip: Treat your wallet like your digital vault. The better you protect it, the safer your crypto journey will be. Remember, your private key is the key to your funds. Keep it safe, offline, and away from prying eyes.

By taking a proactive approach to wallet security and understanding the best practices, you can confidently manage your cryptocurrency assets and minimize the risk of loss or theft.

Chapter 3:

How to Buy Your First Cryptocurrency

Why Buying Cryptocurrency Is a Big Step

Congratulations! By setting up your wallet, you've taken your first tangible step into the world of crypto. Now, it's time to fill that wallet with your first cryptocurrency. This chapter will guide you through the process, from choosing the right exchange to making your first purchase safely and confidently.

Buying your first cryptocurrency is a significant milestone. It marks your entry into a decentralized financial system that offers numerous benefits, from financial freedom to investment opportunities. However, it's important to approach this process with caution and knowledge.

In the following sections, we'll delve into the various methods of buying cryptocurrency, the importance of security, and tips for making informed decisions. By following these guidelines, you can ensure a smooth and secure experience as you embark on your crypto journey.

1. Understanding Cryptocurrency Exchanges

A cryptocurrency exchange is a platform where you can buy, sell, and trade cryptocurrencies. Think of it as a digital marketplace where you can exchange traditional currencies like USD or EUR for digital assets like Bitcoin, Ethereum, or other altcoins.

Exchanges come in two main types:

Centralized Exchanges (CEX):

- These exchanges are operated by a central company that facilitates trades between buyers and sellers.
- They often offer a user-friendly interface and a wide range of cryptocurrencies.
- Examples of popular CEXs include Coinbase, Binance, and Kraken.

Decentralized Exchanges (DEX):

- DEXs operate without a central authority, relying on peer-to-peer transactions facilitated by smart contracts.
- They offer greater privacy and security but can be more complex to use for beginners.
- Examples of popular DEXs include Uniswap, PancakeSwap, and Curve Finance.

When choosing an exchange, consider factors such as:

- **Security:** Prioritize exchanges with strong security measures, including two-factor authentication and cold storage for funds.
- **Fees:** Compare trading fees, withdrawal fees, and deposit fees to find the most cost-effective option.
- **User Interface:** A user-friendly interface can make the trading experience more enjoyable, especially for beginners.
- **Supported Cryptocurrencies:** Ensure the exchange offers the cryptocurrencies you're interested in trading.
- **Regulatory Compliance:** Choose a reputable exchange that complies with relevant regulations to mitigate legal risks.

By carefully evaluating these factors, you can select a reliable exchange that suits your needs and helps you navigate the complex world of cryptocurrency trading.

2. Choosing the Right Exchange

For your first purchase, a centralized exchange is often the best choice due to its simplicity and user-friendly interface. Consider the following factors when selecting an exchange:

- **Availability:** Ensure the exchange operates in your country and complies with local regulations.
- **Reputation:** Choose a trusted exchange with a strong track record and positive user reviews.

- **Fees:** Compare trading fees, withdrawal fees, and deposit fees to find the most cost-effective option.
- **Cryptocurrency Selection:** Make sure the exchange offers the cryptocurrency you want to buy. A wider range of supported cryptocurrencies provides more flexibility.
- **Security:** Prioritize exchanges that prioritize security measures, such as two-factor authentication and cold storage for funds.

Popular Options

- **Coinbase:** A user-friendly platform that's ideal for beginners. It offers a wide range of cryptocurrencies, supports fiat currency deposits, and provides educational resources to help you navigate the crypto space.
- **Binance:** A popular exchange known for its extensive selection of cryptocurrencies, competitive fees, and advanced trading features. However, the interface can be more complex for beginners.
- **Kraken:** A reputable exchange that prioritizes security and offers robust features for both beginners and experienced traders. They also have a strong focus on regulatory compliance.
- **Crypto.com:** A versatile platform offering a user-friendly interface, a wide range of cryptocurrencies, and various features like staking and NFT marketplaces. It's a good option for users seeking a one-stop shop for their crypto needs.

- **Gate.io:** A growing exchange known for its competitive fees and support for a vast array of cryptocurrencies. While it offers a user-friendly interface, some advanced features might be more suitable for experienced traders.

Remember to conduct thorough research and read reviews before choosing an exchange. It's also important to be aware of potential risks, such as hacking and phishing attacks. By selecting a reputable exchange and following best practices, you can minimize these risks and ensure a safe and secure trading experience.

3. Funding Your Exchange Account

Before you can buy cryptocurrency, you'll need to fund your exchange account with fiat currency. Most exchanges offer the following options:

- **Bank Transfer:** This is often the cheapest option, as it usually involves minimal fees. However, it can take a few days for the funds to be processed and credited to your account.
- **Credit/Debit Card:** This is a convenient way to deposit funds instantly. However, credit card purchases often incur higher fees than bank transfers.
- **Third-Party Payment Systems:** Some exchanges allow you to deposit funds using third-party payment systems like PayPal or Apple Pay. However, availability may vary depending on your location and the exchange.

Pro Tip: Start with a small deposit to familiarize yourself with the platform and the buying process. Once you're comfortable, you can deposit larger amounts.

Remember to verify your identity by providing the necessary documentation, such as a government-issued ID and proof of address. This is a standard procedure to comply with regulations and prevent fraud.

4. Step-by-Step Guide to Buying Cryptocurrency

Let's walk through the process of buying cryptocurrency on a centralized exchange like Coinbase:

1. Create an Account:

- Sign up on the exchange's website or download the mobile app.
- Complete the required identity verification process, which typically involves submitting a government-issued ID and proof of address.

2. Deposit Funds:

- Choose your preferred deposit method:
    - **Bank Transfer:** This is usually the most cost-effective option, but it can take several business days for the funds to be processed.
    - **Credit/Debit Card:** This is a faster option, but it often comes with higher fees.

- Follow the exchange's instructions to complete the deposit process.

3. Select a Cryptocurrency:

- Browse the list of available cryptocurrencies on the exchange.
- For beginners, Bitcoin (BTC) and Ethereum (ETH) are popular choices.

4. Place an Order:

- **Market Order:** This allows you to buy cryptocurrency at the current market price.
- **Limit Order:** This allows you to set a specific price at which you want to buy the cryptocurrency.

5. Transfer to Your Wallet:

- Once you've purchased the cryptocurrency, you can transfer it to your personal wallet for added security.
- Double-check the wallet address before confirming the transfer to avoid any errors.

Additional Tips:

- **Start Small:** Begin with a small investment to get familiar with the process and the market.
- **Diversify Your Portfolio:** Consider investing in multiple cryptocurrencies to spread risk.

- **Stay Informed:** Keep up-to-date with the latest news and market trends.
- **Be Patient:** The cryptocurrency market can be volatile, so it's important to have a long-term perspective.

By following these steps and keeping in mind the best practices, you can safely and securely purchase cryptocurrency on a centralized exchange.

6. Staying Safe When Buying Cryptocurrency

To ensure a secure and hassle-free experience when buying cryptocurrency, follow these essential tips:

- Use Reputable Exchanges:
    - Choose well-established and regulated exchanges with a strong track record.
    - Avoid unregulated platforms or offers that sound too good to be true, as they may be scams or scams.

- Enable Two-Factor Authentication (2FA):
    - Add an extra layer of security to your account by enabling 2FA. This typically involves receiving a code via SMS or authenticator app to verify your identity.

- Avoid Public Wi-Fi:

- Always use a secure internet connection when accessing your exchange account or transferring funds. Public Wi-Fi networks are vulnerable to hacking attempts.

- **Transfer to Your Wallet:**
    - Never leave large amounts of cryptocurrency on an exchange for extended periods.
    - Transfer your funds to a secure personal wallet to minimize the risk of loss or theft.

- **Be Wary of Phishing Attacks:**
    - Be cautious of phishing emails, messages, or websites that may try to steal your login credentials or private keys.
    - Always verify the authenticity of the website or email address before entering any sensitive information.

By following these guidelines, you can significantly reduce the risk of cyberattacks and protect your cryptocurrency investments. Remember, security is paramount in the world of cryptocurrency, so prioritize it at all times.

7. Which Cryptocurrency Should You Buy First?

If you're unsure which cryptocurrency to start with, here are some beginner-friendly options:

- **Bitcoin (BTC):** As the first and most well-known cryptocurrency, Bitcoin is often considered a safe and reliable investment. It's known for its strong community, robust technology, and potential as a store of value.
- **Ethereum (ETH):** Ethereum is a versatile blockchain platform that powers a wide range of decentralized applications, including DeFi, NFTs, and gaming. It's a good choice for those interested in the broader ecosystem of blockchain technology.
- **Vector Smart Gas (VSG):** VSG, the native token of VSC, Vector Smart Chain, A high-performance, flat-fee blockchain that's gaining popularity for its fast transaction speeds and user-friendly experience. VSG is essential for interacting with the ecosystem.
- **Stablecoins (e.g., USDT, USDC):** Stablecoins are cryptocurrencies pegged to fiat currencies like the US dollar. They are less volatile than other cryptocurrencies and can be a good choice for those who want to avoid the price fluctuations associated with other digital assets.

Pro Tip: Avoid chasing hype. Stick with established cryptocurrencies with strong fundamentals and a proven track record. Do your own research and consider factors like market capitalization, team experience, and technology.

Remember, it's important to diversify your portfolio and invest only what you can afford to lose. The cryptocurrency market is highly volatile, and prices can fluctuate significantly.

8. Common Mistakes to Avoid

As you embark on your cryptocurrency journey, it's essential to be aware of common pitfalls and avoid making costly mistakes. Here are some common mistakes to watch out for:

- **Buying Too Much Too Soon:** It's tempting to invest heavily in cryptocurrency, especially during periods of rapid price appreciation. However, it's crucial to start small and gradually increase your investment as you gain more experience and confidence.
- **Falling for Scams:** The cryptocurrency space is rife with scams, from phishing attacks to fraudulent projects. Always be vigilant, double-check URLs, and avoid unsolicited offers.
- **Ignoring Security:** Never share your private keys or seed phrase with anyone. Use strong, unique passwords and enable two-factor authentication whenever possible. Be cautious of phishing attacks and avoid clicking on suspicious links or downloading malicious software.

By avoiding these common mistakes, you can protect your investments and ensure a safer and more rewarding cryptocurrency experience. Remember, patience, diligence, and a strong focus on security are key to long-term success in the crypto world.

WTF Does It All Mean?

Buying your first cryptocurrency is an exciting milestone. It's not just about owning digital money—it's about taking part in a revolutionary financial system. By choosing a reputable exchange, starting small, and prioritizing security, you'll set yourself up for a successful journey into the world of crypto.

In the next chapter, we'll explore how to build a beginner's portfolio and start managing your investments effectively. We'll discuss diversification strategies, risk management techniques, and how to stay updated on market trends.

Pro Tip: Treat your first purchase as a learning experience. The more you practice and experiment, the more confident you'll become in navigating the crypto market. Remember, the journey of a thousand miles begins with a single step. So, take that first step and embrace the exciting world of cryptocurrency.

Chapter 4:

Building a Beginner's Portfolio

Why Building a Portfolio Matters

Once you've purchased your first cryptocurrency, it's tempting to keep buying more of the same. However, building a diverse portfolio is a key strategy for managing risk and maximizing potential returns. A well-balanced portfolio can help you navigate the volatile world of crypto with greater confidence and stability.

By diversifying your investments across different cryptocurrencies, you can spread risk and reduce your exposure to the fluctuations of any single asset. Additionally, a diversified portfolio can provide exposure to a variety of innovative projects and technologies, increasing your potential for long-term growth.

In the following sections, we'll discuss the importance of diversification, how to assess risk, and strategies for building a balanced cryptocurrency portfolio. By following these guidelines, you can create a portfolio that aligns with your investment goals and risk tolerance.

1. The Importance of Diversification

Diversification means spreading your investments across different cryptocurrencies to reduce the impact of a single asset's poor performance.

Why It's Important:

- **Reduces Risk:** By investing in a variety of cryptocurrencies, you can mitigate the risk of significant losses. If one asset declines in value, others may perform well, helping to offset the losses.
- **Covers Different Use Cases:** Each cryptocurrency serves a unique purpose, from facilitating payments to powering decentralized applications. Diversifying your portfolio allows you to benefit from the growth potential of different sectors within the crypto ecosystem.

Example:

- **Bitcoin (BTC):** Often referred to as "digital gold," Bitcoin is known for its stability and potential as a store of value.
- **Ethereum (ETH):** As the leading smart contract platform, Ethereum powers a wide range of decentralized applications, including DeFi and NFTs.

- **Solana (SOL):** This high-performance blockchain offers fast transaction speeds and low fees, making it ideal for various applications, including gaming and decentralized finance.

By diversifying your portfolio, you can increase your chances of long-term success in the cryptocurrency market. Remember, diversification doesn't guarantee profits, but it can help you manage risk and potentially increase your overall returns.

2. Types of Cryptocurrencies to Include

To build a well-diversified portfolio, consider including the following types of cryptocurrencies:

1. Blue-Chip Cryptocurrencies:

- Established assets with a strong track record.
- Examples: Bitcoin (BTC), Ethereum (ETH)
- **Why Include Them:** These cryptocurrencies have a proven track record and are less volatile than newer altcoins. They offer a relatively stable investment option and can serve as a foundation for your portfolio.

2. Altcoins:

- Cryptocurrencies other than Bitcoin.
- Examples: Cardano (ADA), Polygon (MATIC), Vector Smart Gas (VSG)
- **Why Include Them:** Altcoins have the potential for higher returns, as they are often associated with

innovative technologies and emerging use cases. However, they also carry higher risk due to their volatility and uncertainty.

3. Stablecoins:

- **Cryptocurrencies pegged to stable assets like the US dollar.**
- **Examples:** USDT (Tether), USDC (USD Coin)
- **Why Include Them:** Stablecoins can help reduce portfolio volatility and provide liquidity for trading other cryptocurrencies. They can also be used as a safe haven during market downturns.

4. Niche Tokens:

- **Tokens targeting specific industries or use cases.**
- **Examples:** Chainlink (LINK) for data oracles, Axie Infinity (AXS) for gaming
- **Why Include Them:** Niche tokens can offer high-risk, high-reward opportunities. However, it's important to conduct thorough research and understand the underlying technology and use case before investing.

Remember to carefully assess your risk tolerance and investment goals before allocating funds to different types of cryptocurrencies. A well-diversified portfolio can help you manage risk and maximize potential returns.

3. Allocating Your Portfolio

A good starting point for beginners is the 60/30/10 rule:

- **60% Blue-Chip Cryptocurrencies:** Invest in established and well-established cryptocurrencies like Bitcoin (BTC) and Ethereum (ETH). These coins have a proven track record and are less volatile than newer altcoins.
- **30% Altcoins:** Allocate a portion of your portfolio to promising altcoins with high growth potential. This could include projects like Solana (SOL), Cardano (ADA), or Polkadot (DOT), which offer unique features and innovative technologies.
- **10% High-Risk Tokens:** Consider investing a small portion of your portfolio in high-risk, high-reward tokens. These could include new projects, meme coins, or tokens with speculative potential. However, be aware that these investments carry higher risk and volatility.

Pro Tip: Adjust these percentages based on your risk tolerance and investment goals. If you're more risk-averse, you might allocate a higher percentage to blue-chip cryptocurrencies. If you're comfortable with higher risk, you can increase your allocation to altcoins and high-risk tokens.

Remember, it's important to conduct thorough research and due diligence before investing in any cryptocurrency. Stay informed about market trends, technological advancements, and regulatory developments. Additionally, consider consulting with a financial advisor to get personalized advice.

4. Tools for Managing Your Portfolio

Keeping track of your investments is crucial for informed decision-making. Here are some tools to help you manage your cryptocurrency portfolio:

Portfolio Tracking Apps:

- **CoinStats:** This comprehensive app allows you to track your portfolio across multiple exchanges and wallets. It provides real-time price updates, historical performance charts, and personalized insights.
- **CoinGecko:** While primarily a cryptocurrency data aggregator, CoinGecko offers portfolio tracking features, allowing you to monitor your holdings and set up price alerts.
- **Delta:** This user-friendly app provides detailed portfolio tracking, tax reporting, and personalized insights. It also offers features like price alerts and portfolio performance benchmarks.

Wallet Integration:

Many popular cryptocurrency wallets, such as MetaMask and Trust Wallet, offer built-in portfolio tracking features. You can view your token balances, transaction history, and even set up price alerts directly within the wallet.

Spreadsheets:

For a more hands-on approach, you can create a simple spreadsheet to track your purchases, average costs, and returns. This allows you to customize your tracking and analysis to your specific needs.

By utilizing these tools, you can gain valuable insights into your portfolio's performance and make informed decisions about your investment strategy.

5. Dollar-Cost Averaging (DCA)

Dollar-cost averaging (DCA) is a simple yet effective investment strategy that involves investing a fixed amount of money in an asset at regular intervals, regardless of the asset's price. This strategy can help you reduce the impact of market volatility and potentially increase your long-term returns.

How DCA Works:

- **Regular Investments:** You invest a fixed amount of money, such as $100, in a particular cryptocurrency at regular intervals, like weekly or monthly.
- **Averaging Out Price Fluctuations:** By investing consistently, you buy more units of the cryptocurrency when the price is low and fewer units when the price is high.
- **Reduced Volatility Impact:** Over time, this strategy can help you achieve a lower average cost per unit, reducing

the impact of market fluctuations on your overall investment.

Why DCA is Beneficial:

- **Emotional Discipline:** DCA helps you avoid impulsive decisions based on short-term price movements.
- **Risk Management:** By spreading your purchases over time, you reduce the risk of investing a large sum at an unfavorable price point.
- **Long-Term Perspective:** DCA encourages a long-term investment approach, which is crucial for success in the volatile cryptocurrency market.

By implementing a DCA strategy, you can take a more disciplined and systematic approach to investing in cryptocurrency. Remember, while DCA can be a helpful strategy, it's important to conduct thorough research and consider your individual financial goals before making investment decisions.

6. Avoiding Common Pitfalls

As you embark on your cryptocurrency investment journey, it's crucial to be aware of common pitfalls and take steps to avoid them:

- **Overconcentration:** Don't put all your money into one cryptocurrency, even if it's popular. Diversify your portfolio to spread risk and maximize potential returns.

- **FOMO (Fear of Missing Out):** Avoid chasing hype or investing in coins just because they're trending. Conduct thorough research and make informed decisions based on fundamentals, not emotions.
- **Neglecting Research:** Always research a project's team, technology, and use case before investing. Look for projects with experienced teams, innovative technology, and strong community support.
- **Ignoring Security Best Practices:** Protect your wallet and private keys to avoid hacking attempts and unauthorized access. Use strong passwords, enable two-factor authentication, and be cautious of phishing scams.
- **Emotional Trading:** Avoid making impulsive decisions based on fear or greed. Stick to your investment plan and avoid selling in panic or buying at the peak of a bull market.

By being mindful of these common pitfalls, you can make more informed investment decisions and protect your assets. Remember, the cryptocurrency market is highly volatile, so it's important to approach investing with a long-term perspective and a disciplined mindset.

7. Researching Cryptocurrencies

Before adding a new cryptocurrency to your portfolio, it's crucial to conduct thorough research. Consider the following factors:

Project Fundamentals:

- **Purpose:** What problem does the cryptocurrency aim to solve? A clear and well-defined use case can indicate a strong project with potential for growth.
- **Technology:** Evaluate the underlying technology of the blockchain. Is it scalable, secure, and energy-efficient? A robust technology stack can enhance the project's long-term viability.
- **Team:** A strong and experienced team can significantly impact the success of a project. Research the team members' backgrounds, expertise, and track record.
- **Community:** A large and active community can provide support, feedback, and contribute to the project's development. Consider the level of community engagement and the quality of discussions.

Market Analysis:

- **Market Cap and Trading Volume:** Analyze the market capitalization and trading volume of the cryptocurrency to gauge its popularity and liquidity.
- **Price History:** Review the historical price performance of the cryptocurrency to identify trends and potential future movements.
- **Tokenomics:** Understand the token's supply, distribution, and economic model. A well-designed tokenomics model can incentivize user adoption and drive long-term value.

Risk Assessment:

- **Volatility:** Cryptocurrencies are known for their volatility. Assess your risk tolerance and be prepared for price fluctuations.
- **Regulatory Risks:** Consider the regulatory environment and potential legal risks associated with the cryptocurrency.
- **Technical Risks:** Evaluate the security of the blockchain and the potential for technical issues.

By conducting thorough research and considering these factors, you can make informed decisions about which cryptocurrencies to add to your portfolio. Remember, it's important to diversify your investments and avoid putting all your eggs in one basket.

8. Rebalancing Your Portfolio

As the market fluctuates, your portfolio's allocations may shift away from your original target percentages. Rebalancing ensures that you maintain your desired risk level and asset allocation.

When to Rebalance:

- **Regular Intervals:** Rebalance your portfolio every 3-6 months, or more frequently during periods of high volatility.

- **Significant Market Movements:** If the market experiences a significant event, such as a bull or bear run, you may need to rebalance sooner to adjust your exposure.

How to Rebalance:

1. **Assess Your Portfolio:** Review your current portfolio allocation and compare it to your target allocation.
2. **Identify Imbalances:** Determine which assets are overweighted or underweighted relative to your target allocation.
3. **Rebalance:** Sell a portion of overperforming assets and use the proceeds to buy underperforming assets.

Benefits of Rebalancing:

- **Risk Management:** Rebalancing can help you manage risk by preventing excessive exposure to any one asset class.
- **Opportunity Seizing:** By selling overvalued assets and buying undervalued ones, you can capitalize on market inefficiencies.
- **Disciplined Investing:** Regular rebalancing can help you maintain a disciplined investment approach and avoid emotional decision-making.

Remember, rebalancing is a strategic approach to portfolio management. By regularly reviewing and adjusting your portfolio, you can improve your long-term investment outcomes.

9. Staying Updated

The cryptocurrency market is dynamic and constantly evolving. To stay informed and make informed decisions, consider the following:

- **Follow Trusted News Sources:** Stay updated with the latest news and developments by following reputable crypto news outlets like CoinDesk, CoinTelegraph, and Cointelegraph. These platforms provide in-depth analysis, market trends, and expert opinions.
- **Join Crypto Communities:** Engage with other crypto enthusiasts on platforms like Reddit, Twitter, and Discord. Participate in discussions, ask questions, and learn from experienced community members.
- **Monitor Market Trends:** Keep an eye on market trends, such as price movements, trading volume, and market sentiment. Use tools like CoinMarketCap and CoinGecko to track the performance of different cryptocurrencies.
- **Stay Informed About Regulatory Developments:** Crypto regulations are constantly changing, so it's important to stay informed about the latest developments in your region. This can impact the availability of certain cryptocurrencies and exchanges.

- **Learn About Technical Analysis and Fundamental Analysis:** These techniques can help you analyze market trends and identify potential investment opportunities.

By staying informed and continuously learning, you can make more informed decisions and navigate the complex world of cryptocurrency with confidence.

WTF Does It All Mean?

Building a portfolio is like planting a garden—you start with a strong foundation, diversify your seeds, and nurture your investments over time. By balancing stability with growth opportunities, you can position yourself for long-term success in the crypto market.

In the next chapter, we'll explore "Staying Safe in the Crypto World," covering essential strategies to protect your investments from scams and fraud. We'll delve into topics like security best practices, recognizing scams, and understanding the importance of staying informed.

Pro Tip: Think of your portfolio as a reflection of your goals and risk tolerance. Start small, stay consistent, and always keep learning. The cryptocurrency market is constantly evolving, so it's important to adapt to changing conditions and embrace new opportunities. By following a disciplined investment approach and staying informed, you can maximize your potential for growth and minimize your risk.

Chapter 5:

Staying Safe in the Crypto World

Why Security Is Critical

The crypto world offers exciting opportunities, but it's also a space where scams, hacks, and fraud are prevalent. Staying safe isn't just about protecting your investments—it's about ensuring you can confidently navigate this new financial frontier.

This chapter will teach you the best practices for safeguarding your assets, recognizing scams, and maintaining your privacy. By following these guidelines, you can significantly reduce your risk and protect your hard-earned money.

In the following sections, we'll delve into specific security measures, common scams to watch out for, and tips for maintaining your privacy in the digital age. Remember, your security is paramount, so take the time to learn and implement these best practices.

1. Common Crypto Scams and Threats

The first step to staying safe is understanding the common risks:

Phishing Attacks:

- Scammers create fake websites or emails that mimic trusted platforms like exchanges or wallet providers.
- They trick users into entering their login credentials or seed phrases, gaining access to their accounts and funds.
- **Example:** A fake MetaMask website that prompts you to enter your seed phrase.

Rug Pulls:

- Developers create a new cryptocurrency project, raise funds from investors, and then abruptly abandon the project, leaving investors with worthless tokens.
- **Example:** A token with no real use case or a team with no transparency.

Ponzi Schemes:

- Scammers promise high returns to early investors, using funds from new investors to pay off old ones.
- As the number of new investors dwindles, the scheme collapses, leaving many people with losses.

Fake Airdrops:

- Scammers offer free cryptocurrency in exchange for personal information or access to your wallet.
- Once they have your information, they can steal your funds or use your identity for malicious purposes.

Hacks:

- Crypto exchanges, wallets, and blockchain platforms can be targeted by hackers who exploit vulnerabilities in their systems.
- Successful hacks can result in significant financial losses for users.

By being aware of these common scams and threats, you can take steps to protect yourself and your investments.

2. Best Practices for Securing Your Crypto

To protect your cryptocurrency investments, follow these best practices:

Protect Your Private Key and Seed Phrase:

- **Never share your private key or seed phrase with anyone, not even support teams.** These are the keys to your cryptocurrency wallet, and compromising them could lead to significant financial loss.

- **Store them offline in a secure location.** Consider using a fireproof safe or a physical storage device like a metal seed phrase recovery kit.

Enable Two-Factor Authentication (2FA):

- **Enable 2FA on your exchange and wallet accounts.** This adds an extra layer of security by requiring a second verification step, such as a code sent to your phone or authenticator app.
- **Use authenticator apps like Google Authenticator or Authy** instead of SMS-based 2FA, as SMS codes can be vulnerable to SIM-swapping attacks.

Choose Reputable Platforms:

- **Use well-known and reputable wallets and exchanges.** Research the platform's security track record and user reviews before entrusting your funds.
- **Avoid using unknown or poorly-reviewed platforms.**

Secure Your Devices:

- **Keep your software and operating systems updated.** Regular updates often include security patches that address vulnerabilities.
- **Use antivirus software** to protect your devices from malware and other threats.
- **Avoid downloading unknown files or apps** from untrusted sources.

Avoid Public Wi-Fi:

- Only access your wallet or exchange accounts on secure, private networks. Public Wi-Fi networks are often vulnerable to hacking attempts.
- Consider using a Virtual Private Network (VPN) to encrypt your internet traffic and add an extra layer of security.

Diversify Storage:

- Don't store all your cryptocurrency in one wallet or on one platform.
- Use a mix of hot wallets for daily use and cold wallets for long-term storage. This helps to reduce the risk of loss in case of a hack or other security breach.

By following these best practices, you can significantly reduce the risk of losing your cryptocurrency to theft or fraud. Remember, security is an ongoing process, so stay informed and adapt your security measures as needed.

3. Red Flags to Watch Out For

Recognizing warning signs can save you from scams and financial loss. Here are some common red flags to watch out for:

- **Unrealistic Promises:** Be wary of projects that promise unrealistic returns or guarantee profits. Legitimate projects often have realistic expectations and avoid making exaggerated claims.

- **Lack of Transparency:** A lack of transparency is a major red flag. Look for projects with clear whitepapers, transparent roadmaps, and identifiable team members. Avoid projects that are shrouded in mystery or have anonymous teams.
- **Urgency Tactics:** Scammers often use high-pressure tactics to manipulate you into making quick decisions. Be cautious of messages urging you to act immediately or miss out on a limited-time opportunity.
- **Unverified Social Media Links:** Always double-check the authenticity of links, especially those shared on social media. Avoid clicking on suspicious links or downloading attachments from unknown sources.
- **Pump-and-Dump Schemes:** These schemes involve artificially inflating the price of a cryptocurrency through coordinated buying and selling, then dumping the tokens to profit from the price increase. Be wary of sudden price surges and excessive hype.
- **Phishing Attacks:** Scammers may send phishing emails or messages that mimic legitimate platforms to steal your personal information or cryptocurrency. Always verify the sender's identity and avoid clicking on suspicious links.

By being aware of these red flags and practicing caution, you can protect yourself from scams and make informed investment decisions. Remember, if something seems too good to be true, it probably is.

4. Safely Navigating Exchanges and Platforms

When using exchanges or crypto platforms, it's crucial to prioritize security:

- **Stick to Reputable Exchanges:** Choose well-established and regulated exchanges with a strong track record. Avoid using unknown or unregulated platforms that may be more susceptible to hacks and scams.
- **Check for SSL Certificates:** Ensure the website you're visiting has a valid SSL certificate, indicated by "https://" in the URL and a padlock icon in your browser's address bar. This helps protect your data from being intercepted during transmission.
- **Enable Two-Factor Authentication (2FA):** This adds an extra layer of security to your account by requiring a second verification step, such as a code sent to your phone or authenticator app.
- **Enable Withdrawal Whitelists:** Restrict withdrawals to pre-approved wallet addresses to prevent unauthorized access to your funds.
- **Beware of Impersonators:** Never share your private keys, seed phrases, or other sensitive information with anyone, including customer support representatives. Scammers may impersonate legitimate support agents to steal your funds.

- **Use Strong, Unique Passwords:** Create strong, unique passwords for each of your exchange accounts. Avoid using easily guessable passwords and consider using a password manager to generate and store complex passwords.
- **Be Wary of Phishing Attacks:** Be cautious of phishing emails, messages, or websites that may attempt to trick you into revealing your personal information or login credentials. Always verify the sender's identity and avoid clicking on suspicious links.

By following these security best practices, you can significantly reduce the risk of losing your cryptocurrency to hackers or scammers. Remember, security is an ongoing process, so stay informed about the latest threats and take proactive steps to protect your assets.

5. Performing Due Diligence on Projects

Before investing in a cryptocurrency or project, it's crucial to conduct thorough due diligence. This involves carefully researching the project's team, technology, community, and financial health. Here are some key factors to consider:

Team:

- **Experience and Expertise:** Assess the experience and qualifications of the team members. A strong, experienced team is more likely to deliver on their promises.

- **Transparency:** Look for transparency in the team's identities and their involvement in the project. A transparent team builds trust with the community.

Technology:

- **Whitepaper:** A well-written whitepaper outlines the project's goals, technology, and roadmap. It should be clear, concise, and free of technical jargon.
- **Smart Contracts:** If the project relies on smart contracts, ensure they are audited by reputable security firms to identify and address potential vulnerabilities.
- **Scalability:** A scalable blockchain can handle increasing transaction volume and maintain low fees.
- **Security:** A robust security infrastructure is essential to protect the project from hacks and other cyber threats.

Community:

- **Active Community:** A strong and active community is a positive sign. A large and engaged community can provide support, feedback, and contribute to the project's development.
- **Social Media Presence:** Monitor the project's social media channels for updates, announcements, and community engagement.

Financial Health:

- **Tokenomics:** Understand the project's tokenomics, including the token supply, distribution, and utility.
- **Funding:** Evaluate the project's funding sources and financial stability.
- **Market Cap and Trading Volume:** Consider the project's market capitalization and trading volume to assess its liquidity and potential for growth.

By conducting thorough due diligence, you can make informed investment decisions and minimize your risk exposure. Remember, investing in cryptocurrency involves inherent risks, and it's important to only invest what you can afford to lose.

6. Recovering from a Security Breach

If your wallet or exchange account is compromised, act quickly to minimize the damage. Here are some steps you can take to recover from a security breach:

1. Assess the Damage:

- **Identify the Compromised Account:** Determine which wallet or exchange account has been affected.
- **Check Transaction History:** Review your transaction history to identify any unauthorized transactions.
- **Estimate Losses:** Calculate the amount of cryptocurrency lost due to the breach.

2. Secure Your Remaining Funds:

- **Transfer Funds to a Secure Wallet:** Move any remaining funds to a secure, offline wallet to prevent further loss.
- **Enable Two-Factor Authentication:** Enable 2FA on all your accounts to add an extra layer of security.
- **Use Strong, Unique Passwords:** Avoid using weak or easily guessable passwords.

3. Report the Incident:

- **Contact the Exchange or Wallet Provider:** Report the incident to the relevant customer support team and provide as much information as possible.
- **File a Police Report:** If you suspect a crime has been committed, file a report with local law enforcement.
- **Engage with the Crypto Community:** Share your experience with other users and warn them about potential scams or security threats.

4. Learn from the Experience:

- **Review Your Security Practices:** Identify any weaknesses in your security measures and take steps to improve them.
- **Stay Informed:** Keep up-to-date with the latest security threats and best practices.
- **Be Wary of Phishing Attempts:** Avoid clicking on suspicious links or downloading attachments from unknown sources.

While recovering from a security breach can be stressful, it's important to stay calm and take decisive action. By following these steps, you can minimize the damage and protect your remaining assets. Remember, prevention is always better than cure, so prioritize security and be vigilant.

7. Staying Informed

The crypto space evolves rapidly, and so do the threats. Staying informed is crucial to navigate this dynamic landscape and protect yourself from scams and security breaches. Here are some tips to stay updated:

- **Follow Trusted News Outlets:** Follow reputable crypto news outlets like CoinDesk, The Block, CoinTelegraph, and Crypto News for the latest news, analysis, and market trends.
- **Join Crypto Communities:** Participate in online forums and communities on platforms like Reddit, Twitter, and Telegram. Engage with other crypto enthusiasts, ask questions, and learn from experienced users.
- **Subscribe to Crypto Newsletters:** Sign up for newsletters from reputable crypto news outlets and exchanges. This will help you stay informed about the latest market trends, regulatory updates, and security alerts.
- **Attend Crypto Conferences and Webinars:** Participate in industry conferences and webinars to learn from experts, network with other crypto enthusiasts, and gain valuable insights.

- **Follow Influential Figures:** Follow thought leaders, analysts, and developers on social media to get their perspectives on market trends and emerging technologies.

By staying informed and engaged with the crypto community, you can make more informed decisions and protect yourself from scams and security threats. Remember, knowledge is power in the world of cryptocurrency.

8. Building a Safety Checklist

Before making any transaction or engaging with a project, it's essential to ask yourself the following questions:

- Is the Platform Secure and Reputable?
    - Stick to well-established and reputable exchanges and wallets.
    - Look for platforms with strong security measures, such as two-factor authentication and cold storage.
    - Research the platform's reputation and read user reviews.

- Have I Verified the Wallet Address Multiple Times?
    - Double-check the wallet address before sending any funds to avoid sending them to the wrong address.

- o Consider using a QR code scanner to verify the address and reduce the risk of typos.

- **Am I Using a Secure, Private Network?**

    - o Avoid using public Wi-Fi networks to access your crypto accounts.
    - o Use a secure, private network to protect your sensitive information from potential hackers.

- **Does the Project Have Transparent Goals and a Credible Team?**

    - o Research the project's whitepaper, team members, and community.
    - o Look for transparency in the project's roadmap and development progress.
    - o Be wary of projects that make unrealistic promises or have anonymous teams.

By following these guidelines and maintaining a vigilant approach, you can significantly reduce the risk of falling victim to scams and security breaches. Remember, when it comes to cryptocurrency, security is paramount.

WTF Does It All Mean?

Safety is the foundation of your crypto journey. By following these best practices and staying vigilant, you can protect your investments and enjoy the many opportunities this space offers.

Remember, in the crypto world, you are your own bank—and with that power comes responsibility.

In the next chapter, we'll explore "How to Use Cryptocurrency in Your Everyday Life," covering topics like making payments, earning passive income through staking and lending, and utilizing decentralized finance (DeFi) protocols.

Pro Tip: Treat every transaction and investment with caution, and never stop learning. The more you understand the underlying technology and the evolving landscape of cryptocurrency, the safer and more confident you'll become. Stay informed, stay curious, and embrace the exciting possibilities that the crypto world has to offer.

Chapter 6:

Exploring Use Cases

Why Use Cases Matter

Cryptocurrency isn't just a digital currency; it's a transformative technology with applications far beyond financial transactions. Understanding these use cases helps you see the bigger picture of how blockchain and crypto are changing the world.

In this chapter, we'll explore the most exciting and practical use cases for cryptocurrency, from payments to decentralized finance and beyond. By understanding these applications, you can appreciate the full potential of this revolutionary technology and its impact on various industries.

From streamlining cross-border payments to empowering individuals with financial freedom, cryptocurrency is poised to revolutionize the way we interact with money and technology. Let's delve into the exciting possibilities that lie ahead.

1. Everyday Payments and Remittances

Cryptocurrencies like Bitcoin (BTC) and stablecoins such as USDT (Tether) are increasingly being used for everyday payments.

Why It Matters:

- **Borderless Transactions:** Cryptocurrencies enable seamless cross-border payments, bypassing traditional banking systems and their associated fees and delays.
- **Lower Fees:** Crypto transactions often involve significantly lower fees compared to traditional payment methods, especially for international transfers.
- **Speed:** Crypto transactions can be processed and confirmed within minutes, providing faster settlement times than traditional banking systems.
- **Accessibility:** Cryptocurrencies can provide financial inclusion to people who are unbanked or underbanked, allowing them to participate in the global economy.

Example:

A freelancer in India can receive payment in USDC from a client in the US without going through an expensive international wire transfer. This can save time and money for both parties.

As the adoption of cryptocurrencies continues to grow, we can expect to see more and more everyday use cases emerge. From paying for goods and services to sending remittances to loved ones, cryptocurrencies have the potential to revolutionize the way we interact with money.

2. Decentralized Finance (DeFi)

DeFi, or Decentralized Finance, is a blockchain-based ecosystem of financial services that operates without traditional banks or intermediaries.

Use Cases:

- **Lending and Borrowing:** Platforms like Aave and Compound allow you to lend your crypto assets and earn interest, or borrow against your holdings as collateral.
- **Yield Farming:** By providing liquidity to decentralized exchanges (DEXs), you can earn rewards in the form of fees or tokens.
- **Decentralized Trading:** Platforms like Uniswap and Vector DEX enable peer-to-peer trading of cryptocurrencies without the need for a centralized exchange.
- **Insurance:** DeFi protocols offer decentralized insurance solutions, protecting users from various risks like smart contract failures or hacks.

Why It Matters:

- **Accessibility:** DeFi is accessible to anyone with an internet connection, regardless of their geographic location or financial background.

- **Transparency:** All transactions and protocols are recorded on a public blockchain, ensuring transparency and accountability.
- **Financial Inclusion:** DeFi can empower individuals and communities by providing access to financial services that may not be available through traditional channels.

Example:

A user can lend their stablecoins on a DeFi platform like Aave and earn interest at a higher rate than a traditional savings account. The interest is paid in the form of the platform's native token, which can be held or used for further DeFi activities.

DeFi has the potential to revolutionize the financial industry by offering innovative solutions and greater financial freedom. However, it's important to be aware of the risks associated with DeFi, such as smart contract vulnerabilities and market volatility.

3. NFTs (Non-Fungible Tokens)

NFTs, or Non-Fungible Tokens, represent unique digital assets on a blockchain. They are revolutionizing industries like art, gaming, and collectibles by enabling the ownership and trading of digital items.

Use Cases:

- **Digital Art:** Artists can sell their digital artwork as NFTs, ensuring authenticity and enabling them to earn royalties on secondary sales.
- **Gaming:** NFTs can represent in-game items like characters, weapons, or virtual land, allowing players to own and trade them.
- **Collectibles:** Physical collectibles like trading cards or sports memorabilia can be tokenized as NFTs, creating a digital record of ownership and authenticity.
- **Real Estate:** Real estate assets can be tokenized, allowing for fractional ownership and easier trading.
- **Music and Entertainment:** Musicians and artists can sell their music, videos, or exclusive experiences as NFTs, directly connecting with fans and earning royalties.

Why It Matters:

- **Ownership:** NFTs provide verifiable ownership of digital assets, ensuring that creators and collectors can maintain control over their creations.
- **Authenticity:** Blockchain technology enables the creation of a permanent and tamper-proof record of ownership, preventing counterfeiting and fraud.
- **Royalties:** NFTs can be programmed to automatically pay royalties to creators whenever their work is resold, ensuring fair compensation for artists and creators.

- **New Revenue Streams:** NFTs open up new revenue streams for artists, musicians, and content creators, allowing them to monetize their work directly with fans.

By understanding the potential of NFTs, you can explore exciting opportunities to create, collect, and invest in digital assets.

4. Supply Chain and Logistics

Blockchain is revolutionizing supply chain management by increasing transparency, efficiency, and trust.

Use Cases:

- **Product Tracking:** By recording the movement of goods on a blockchain, companies can track the journey of products from production to delivery. This transparency helps identify potential bottlenecks, reduce delays, and improve overall efficiency.
- **Authenticity Verification:** Blockchain can be used to verify the authenticity of products, especially luxury goods and organic food. By tracking the product's origin and history, companies can prevent counterfeiting and build consumer trust.
- **Streamlined Payments:** Cryptocurrencies can facilitate faster and more secure payments between suppliers and buyers in the supply chain. Smart contracts can automate payment processes, reducing the need for intermediaries and minimizing the risk of fraud.

Why It Matters:

- **Reduced Fraud and Counterfeiting:** By providing a transparent and immutable record of product provenance, blockchain helps to combat fraud and counterfeiting.
- **Increased Consumer Trust:** Blockchain-powered supply chain solutions can build consumer trust by providing transparency and traceability.
- **Improved Efficiency:** By automating processes and reducing paperwork, blockchain can streamline supply chain operations and reduce costs.
- **Enhanced Sustainability:** Blockchain can be used to track the environmental impact of products, promoting sustainable practices and ethical sourcing.

Example:

A coffee company can use blockchain to track the journey of its coffee beans from the farm to the consumer's cup. By recording information about the origin, processing, and transportation of the beans, the company can provide consumers with greater transparency and traceability. This can help build brand loyalty and differentiate the company from competitors.

As blockchain technology continues to advance, we can expect to see even more innovative applications in the supply chain and logistics industry. By leveraging the power of blockchain, businesses can improve efficiency, reduce costs, and build stronger relationships with their customers.

5. Identity and Data Management

Blockchain enables individuals to own and control their digital identities.

Use Cases:

- **Digital IDs:** Blockchain-based digital IDs can provide a secure and verifiable way to prove identity online, reducing the risk of identity theft and fraud.
- **Data Privacy:** By storing personal data on a blockchain, individuals can grant selective access to specific pieces of information, giving them greater control over their privacy.
- **KYC and Compliance:** Blockchain technology can streamline the Know Your Customer (KYC) and compliance processes for banks and other financial institutions. By securely storing and verifying identity information, blockchain can reduce costs and improve efficiency.

Why It Matters:

- **Enhanced Privacy and Security:** Blockchain-based identity solutions can protect personal information from data breaches and unauthorized access.
- **Elimination of Centralized Data Storage:** By decentralizing identity information, blockchain reduces the risk of data loss or corruption.

- **Efficient and Secure Authentication:** Blockchain-powered digital IDs can streamline authentication processes, making it easier and more secure to access online services.

Example:

A traveler can use a blockchain-based passport to speed through customs and immigration checkpoints without revealing unnecessary personal details. The passport can be securely stored on a mobile device and verified by border control officials.

By leveraging blockchain technology, we can create a more secure, private, and efficient digital identity ecosystem.

6. Tokenized Assets

Tokenization is the process of representing real-world assets, such as real estate, art, or commodities, as digital tokens on a blockchain.

Use Cases:

- **Real Estate:** Tokenization can enable fractional ownership of real estate, allowing individuals to invest in properties that were previously only accessible to wealthy investors.
- **Art and Collectibles:** High-value art pieces and collectibles can be tokenized, making them more accessible to a wider range of investors.

- **Commodities:** Commodities like gold, silver, and oil can be tokenized, providing a more efficient and transparent way to trade these assets.
- **Stocks and Bonds:** Traditional securities can be tokenized, allowing for fractional ownership and easier trading.

Why It Matters:

- **Increased Liquidity:** By breaking down assets into smaller, tokenized units, tokenization can increase liquidity and make them more accessible to a wider range of investors.
- **Democratization of Finance:** Tokenization can democratize access to investments that were previously reserved for high-net-worth individuals and institutions.
- **Efficiency and Transparency:** Blockchain technology can streamline the trading and settlement processes, reducing costs and improving transparency.
- **Innovation:** Tokenization can enable new financial products and services, such as decentralized exchanges, lending platforms, and insurance protocols.

Example:

An investor can buy a fraction of a tokenized luxury apartment for $1,000, gaining exposure to the real estate market without having to invest a significant amount of capital. This fractional ownership model can democratize access to high-value assets and provide greater flexibility and liquidity for investors.

As blockchain technology continues to evolve, we can expect to see a wide range of assets tokenized, opening up new opportunities for investment and innovation.

7. Gaming and Virtual Worlds

Blockchain is reshaping the gaming industry by enabling true ownership of in-game assets.

Use Cases:

- **Play-to-Earn Games:** Players can earn cryptocurrency rewards by completing tasks, winning battles, or participating in virtual economies. This incentivizes players to spend more time in the game and can generate significant income.
- **Virtual Real Estate:** Players can buy, sell, or rent virtual land in blockchain-based virtual worlds like Decentraland or The Sandbox. This allows for the creation of unique virtual experiences and the development of virtual economies.
- **Interoperability:** Blockchain-based gaming platforms can enable interoperability between different games, allowing players to transfer their in-game assets and characters across multiple titles.

Why It Matters:

- **Player Empowerment:** Blockchain technology empowers players by giving them true ownership of

their in-game assets. This allows players to trade, sell, or use their assets across different games and platforms.
- **New Economic Opportunities:** Blockchain-based gaming can create new economic opportunities for players, developers, and content creators. Players can earn income by playing games, creating in-game assets, or trading on virtual marketplaces.
- **Innovative Gameplay:** Blockchain technology can enable innovative gameplay experiences, such as decentralized autonomous organizations (DAOs) that allow players to govern the game's development and economy.

Example:

A player can earn Axie Infinity Shards (AXS) by playing the popular play-to-earn game Axie Infinity. These tokens can be sold on decentralized exchanges for real-world value, providing players with a potential source of income.

As blockchain technology continues to advance, we can expect to see even more exciting developments in the gaming industry, from immersive virtual worlds to innovative play-to-earn models.

8. Environmental Sustainability

Blockchain technology is being used to combat climate change and promote sustainability.

Use Cases:

- **Carbon Credits:** Blockchain can be used to track and verify carbon credits, making it easier to trade and retire them. This can incentivize businesses to reduce their carbon emissions and invest in sustainable practices.
- **Renewable Energy Certificates:** Blockchain can be used to track the origin and authenticity of renewable energy certificates (RECs), ensuring that they represent genuine renewable energy production.
- **Supply Chain Efficiency:** By tracking the origin and movement of goods on the blockchain, businesses can reduce waste, optimize logistics, and minimize their environmental impact.
- **Sustainable Agriculture:** Blockchain can be used to track the origin and quality of food products, ensuring that they are produced sustainably and ethically.

Why It Matters:

- **Accountability and Transparency:** Blockchain provides a transparent and immutable record of environmental impact, ensuring accountability and preventing fraud.
- **Incentivizing Sustainable Practices:** By rewarding sustainable behavior with carbon credits and other incentives, blockchain can encourage businesses and individuals to adopt eco-friendly practices.

- **Efficient Resource Management:** Blockchain can help optimize resource allocation and reduce waste by tracking the movement of goods and materials.
- **Consumer Empowerment:** By providing consumers with transparent information about the environmental impact of products, blockchain can empower them to make informed choices and support sustainable businesses.

Example:

A company can use blockchain to track the energy consumption of its operations and verify the amount of renewable energy it produces. By sharing this information with consumers, the company can build trust and demonstrate its commitment to sustainability.

By leveraging the power of blockchain, we can create a more sustainable future and address the challenges of climate change.

9. DAOs (Decentralized Autonomous Organizations)

DAOs, or Decentralized Autonomous Organizations, are community-led organizations governed by smart contracts.

Use Cases:

- **Decentralized Governance:** DAOs allow members to vote on proposals and make decisions collectively, without the need for a central authority. This empowers the community to shape the future of the organization.

- **Crowdfunding:** DAOs can be used to raise funds for various projects, from open-source software development to social causes. Members can contribute funds and receive tokens in return, which represent ownership in the project.
- **Incentive Programs:** DAOs can use tokens to incentivize community members to contribute to the project's development and growth. This can include tasks like coding, marketing, or community moderation.

Why It Matters:

- **Empowerment:** DAOs empower individuals to participate in decision-making and contribute to projects they care about.
- **Transparency and Accountability:** All decisions and actions of a DAO are recorded on the blockchain, ensuring transparency and accountability.
- **Innovation:** DAOs can foster innovation by enabling rapid experimentation and the development of new business models.

Example:

A DAO can be formed to fund a renewable energy project, with members contributing funds and receiving tokens in return. The DAO's smart contracts can automate the distribution of rewards based on each member's contribution, ensuring transparency and fairness.

DAOs have the potential to revolutionize the way organizations are structured and operated, enabling more democratic, efficient, and transparent governance models.

WTF Does It All Mean?

Cryptocurrency and blockchain technology are much more than speculative investments—they're tools driving innovation across industries. Whether you're making payments, earning passive income, or exploring virtual worlds, the possibilities are endless.

In the next chapter, we'll discuss "Understanding Trends in Crypto," helping you stay ahead of the curve in this ever-evolving landscape. We'll explore emerging technologies, regulatory developments, and future predictions that will shape the future of cryptocurrency.

Pro Tip: Experiment with different use cases to discover how blockchain can fit into your life or business. By actively engaging with the ecosystem and staying curious, you can unlock the full potential of this revolutionary technology.

Chapter 7:

Understanding Trends in Crypto

Why Keeping Up with Trends Is Important

The crypto landscape evolves at lightning speed. What's hot today might be outdated tomorrow. Staying informed about trends helps you make smarter investment decisions, avoid scams, and capitalize on emerging opportunities.

This chapter explores the key trends shaping the future of cryptocurrency, from decentralized finance to tokenization, and explains why they matter. By understanding these trends, you can position yourself to take advantage of the next big thing in the crypto world.

In the following sections, we'll delve into the latest trends and discuss their potential impact on the future of finance, technology, and society.

1. Decentralized Finance (DeFi): Reinventing Finance

DeFi, or Decentralized Finance, is one of the most transformative trends in crypto, providing decentralized alternatives to traditional financial services.

Key Features:

- **Lending and Borrowing:** DeFi platforms allow users to lend their crypto assets and earn interest, or borrow against their holdings without the need for traditional credit checks.
- **Decentralized Exchanges (DEXs):** DEXs enable peer-to-peer trading of cryptocurrencies without the need for intermediaries. This provides greater transparency, security, and control for users.
- **Yield Farming and Staking:** Users can earn rewards by providing liquidity to decentralized exchanges or staking their tokens to support the network's security.

Why It Matters:

- **Open Finance:** DeFi opens up financial services to anyone with an internet connection, regardless of their location or financial background.
- **Reduced Reliance on Traditional Finance:** By eliminating the need for banks and other intermediaries, DeFi can reduce fees and increase efficiency.
- **Innovation and Experimentation:** The decentralized nature of DeFi enables rapid innovation and

experimentation, leading to the development of new financial products and services.

Emerging Trend: Cross-Chain DeFi

Cross-chain DeFi protocols are emerging, enabling seamless transactions and asset transfers between different blockchains. This interoperability will further expand the DeFi ecosystem and unlock new opportunities for users.

DeFi has the potential to revolutionize the financial industry by providing a more inclusive, transparent, and efficient system. As the technology continues to evolve, we can expect to see even more innovative DeFi applications emerge.

2. NFTs: Beyond Digital Art

NFTs started with digital art and collectibles but are now expanding into other industries.

Emerging Use Cases:

- **Gaming:** NFTs can represent in-game items like characters, weapons, and virtual land, giving players true ownership of their digital assets. This enables players to trade, sell, or rent their in-game items, creating new economic opportunities within the gaming industry.
- **Real Estate:** Real estate properties can be tokenized, allowing for fractional ownership and easier trading. This can democratize access to real estate investments

and open up new opportunities for both investors and property owners.
- **Music and Media:** Artists can release their music, videos, or other digital content as NFTs, providing fans with exclusive access and ownership rights. This can help artists monetize their work directly and build stronger relationships with their audience.
- **Supply Chain and Logistics:** NFTs can be used to track the provenance of products, ensuring authenticity and transparency. This can help reduce counterfeiting and improve supply chain efficiency.

Why It Matters:

- **True Ownership:** NFTs enable true ownership of digital assets, empowering creators and collectors.
- **Transparency and Authenticity:** Blockchain technology ensures transparency and authenticity, preventing fraud and counterfeiting.
- **New Revenue Streams:** NFTs can create new revenue streams for artists, musicians, and content creators, allowing them to directly monetize their work.
- **Innovation and Experimentation:** NFTs are driving innovation and experimentation in various industries, from gaming and art to finance and real estate.

As NFT technology continues to evolve, we can expect to see even more innovative applications emerge, transforming the way we interact with digital assets and the digital world.

3. Layer-1 and Layer-2 Solutions

As blockchain networks grow, scalability and efficiency become critical challenges. To address these issues, the industry has developed innovative solutions at both the Layer-1 and Layer-2 levels.

Layer-1 Blockchains

- **Examples:** Ethereum, Solana, Vector Smart Chain (VSC)
- **Focus:** Layer-1 blockchains focus on improving the core protocol of a blockchain network, such as the consensus mechanism, transaction processing speed, and security.
- **Benefits:** Increased scalability, faster transaction speeds, and lower fees.

Layer-2 Scaling Solutions

- **Examples:** Polygon, Arbitrum, Optimism
- **Focus:** Layer-2 solutions build on top of Layer-1 blockchains to handle transactions off-chain, reducing congestion and fees on the main chain.
- **Benefits:** Improved scalability, faster transaction confirmation times, and lower fees.

Why It Matters:

- **Mass Adoption:** Scalability is essential for mass adoption of blockchain technology. By addressing the limitations

of Layer-1 blockchains, Layer-2 solutions can enable a wider range of applications and users.
- **Cost-Effective Transactions:** Lower transaction fees make blockchain technology more accessible to individuals and businesses.
- **Enhanced User Experience:** Faster transaction speeds and improved scalability can lead to a better user experience.

Emerging Trend: Modular Blockchains

Modular blockchains are a new approach to blockchain architecture that separates different components of the blockchain, such as transaction processing, data storage, and consensus mechanisms. This modular approach allows for greater flexibility and customization, potentially leading to more efficient and scalable blockchain networks.

By understanding the role of Layer-1 and Layer-2 solutions, you can better appreciate the ongoing evolution of blockchain technology and its potential to reshape industries.

4. Institutional Adoption

Institutional interest in cryptocurrency is growing rapidly, legitimizing the market and driving demand.

Key Developments:

- **Corporate Investments:** Major companies like Tesla and MicroStrategy have invested heavily in Bitcoin,

signaling a shift in corporate attitudes towards cryptocurrency.
- **Crypto Custody Services:** Traditional financial institutions, such as banks and asset management firms, are offering crypto custody services, providing secure storage and management of digital assets.
- **Crypto-Focused ETFs and Investment Funds:** The emergence of crypto-focused exchange-traded funds (ETFs) and investment funds has made it easier for institutional investors to allocate capital to the cryptocurrency market.

Why It Matters:

- **Market Stability:** Institutional adoption can help stabilize the cryptocurrency market by providing a steady flow of capital and reducing volatility.
- **Regulatory Clarity:** As more institutions enter the space, it may lead to increased regulatory clarity and a more mature market.
- **Increased Liquidity:** Institutional investment can boost liquidity in the cryptocurrency market, making it easier to buy and sell digital assets.

Emerging Trend: Institutional Adoption of DeFi

Institutional investors are increasingly exploring opportunities within the DeFi ecosystem. By leveraging enterprise blockchain solutions and tokenized assets, institutions can streamline processes, reduce costs, and access new markets.

As institutional adoption continues to grow, the cryptocurrency market is poised for significant growth and mainstream acceptance.

5. Real-World Asset Tokenization

Tokenization is the process of representing real-world assets, such as real estate, art, or commodities, as digital tokens on a blockchain.

How It Works:

- **Asset Digitization:** Real-world assets are divided into smaller, fractionalized units.
- **Token Creation:** Each fractional unit is represented by a unique digital token on a blockchain.
- **Trading and Ownership:** These tokens can be bought, sold, or traded on decentralized exchanges.

Why It Matters:

- **Increased Liquidity:** Tokenization can increase the liquidity of real-world assets, making them more accessible to a wider range of investors.
- **Fractional Ownership:** Tokenization allows for fractional ownership of assets, making it easier for individuals to invest in high-value assets.
- **Transparency and Security:** Blockchain technology ensures transparency and security in the ownership and transfer of assets.

- **Efficient Trading:** Tokenized assets can be traded 24/7 on decentralized exchanges, reducing transaction costs and settlement times.

Emerging Trend: Tokenized Carbon Credits and Renewable Energy Certificates

Tokenizing carbon credits and renewable energy certificates can help track and verify environmental impact, incentivize sustainable practices, and create new investment opportunities.

By tokenizing real-world assets, we can unlock new possibilities for investment, trade, and financial innovation. As blockchain technology continues to evolve, we can expect to see a growing number of asset classes being tokenized, transforming traditional industries and creating new economic opportunities.

6. DAOs (Decentralized Autonomous Organizations)

DAOs, or Decentralized Autonomous Organizations, represent a new way of organizing and governing communities and businesses.

Key Features:

- **Community-Led Governance:** DAOs are governed by their members, who vote on proposals and make decisions collectively.
- **Smart Contract Automation:** Smart contracts automate the execution of rules and agreements, reducing the need for intermediaries and ensuring transparency.

- **Token-Based Incentives:** DAOs often use tokens to incentivize participation and reward contributions to the organization.

Why It Matters:

- **Empowerment:** DAOs empower individuals to participate in decision-making and governance processes.
- **Transparency and Accountability:** All decisions and actions of a DAO are recorded on the blockchain, ensuring transparency and accountability.
- **Innovation:** DAOs can foster innovation by enabling rapid experimentation and the development of new business models.

Emerging Trend: DAOs Managing Real-World Assets and Initiatives

DAOs are increasingly being used to manage real-world assets and initiatives. For example, DAOs can be used to:

- **Fund and manage investment funds:** By pooling resources and making collective investment decisions.
- **Support charitable causes:** By allocating funds to social and environmental projects.
- **Develop and maintain open-source software:** By incentivizing developers and ensuring the long-term sustainability of projects.

DAOs have the potential to revolutionize the way we organize and govern, creating more democratic, efficient, and transparent organizations. As the technology continues to evolve, we can expect to see even more innovative and impactful applications of DAOs.

7. Privacy and Security Enhancements

As more people adopt crypto, privacy and security are becoming top priorities.

Key Innovations:

- **Privacy-Focused Cryptocurrencies:** Cryptocurrencies like Monero and Zcash offer enhanced privacy features, allowing users to conduct transactions without revealing their identities.
- **Zero-Knowledge Proofs (ZKPs):** ZKPs enable the verification of information without revealing the underlying data. This technology can be used to enhance the privacy and security of blockchain transactions.

Why It Matters:

- **Balancing Transparency and Privacy:** Privacy-enhancing technologies allow users to maintain a balance between transparency and personal privacy.
- **Enhancing Trust:** By ensuring the confidentiality of user data, privacy-focused solutions can build trust in blockchain technology.

- **Regulatory Compliance:** Privacy-preserving technologies can help organizations comply with data privacy regulations like GDPR and CCPA.

Emerging Trend: Integration of Privacy Solutions into Mainstream Blockchains

There is a growing trend towards integrating privacy-enhancing technologies into mainstream blockchains like Ethereum. This will allow for more private and secure transactions on these popular platforms.

As the demand for privacy and security in the crypto space continues to grow, we can expect to see further advancements in privacy-enhancing technologies.

8. AI and Blockchain Integration

The combination of artificial intelligence (AI) and blockchain is unlocking new possibilities.

Use Cases:

- **Data Sharing:** AI algorithms can be trained on vast amounts of data stored on blockchain networks, leading to more accurate and insightful models.
- **Smart Contracts:** AI can be used to create more sophisticated smart contracts that can adapt to real-world events and make autonomous decisions.

- **Fraud Detection:** AI-powered tools can analyze blockchain transactions to identify and prevent fraudulent activities.
- **Personalized Finance:** AI-powered dApps can provide personalized financial advice and services based on individual needs and preferences.

Why It Matters:

- **Improved Efficiency:** AI can automate tasks and streamline processes, making blockchain systems more efficient and cost-effective.
- **Enhanced Security:** AI-powered security solutions can help protect blockchain networks from attacks and fraud.
- **Advanced Analytics:** By analyzing large amounts of blockchain data, AI can uncover valuable insights and trends.
- **New Applications:** The integration of AI and blockchain can lead to the development of innovative applications in various industries, such as healthcare, supply chain management, and finance.

Emerging Trend: AI-Driven Decentralized Applications (dApps)

AI-driven dApps can provide personalized financial advice, automate trading strategies, and offer tailored services to users. As AI and blockchain technologies continue to evolve, we can expect to see even more sophisticated and innovative applications emerge.

The integration of AI and blockchain has the potential to revolutionize industries and create a more intelligent, efficient, and secure digital future.

9. Green Blockchain Initiatives

Sustainability is a growing focus in the crypto industry.

Key Innovations:

- **Proof-of-Stake (PoS) Blockchains:** PoS consensus mechanisms consume significantly less energy than traditional Proof-of-Work (PoW) systems. By staking their tokens, users validate transactions and secure the network, eliminating the need for energy-intensive mining operations.
- **Tokenized Carbon Credits:** Carbon credits, which represent reductions in carbon emissions, can be tokenized and traded on blockchain platforms. This can incentivize carbon reduction efforts and facilitate the global carbon market.

Why It Matters:

- **Reduced Environmental Impact:** Green blockchain initiatives aim to reduce the carbon footprint of the cryptocurrency industry and promote sustainable practices.

- **Attracting Eco-Conscious Users:** By prioritizing sustainability, blockchain projects can attract a growing number of environmentally conscious users and investors.
- **Driving Innovation:** Green blockchain technology can enable innovative solutions to address climate change and other environmental challenges.

Emerging Trend: Green Blockchains

Green blockchains are specifically designed to be energy-efficient and environmentally friendly. These blockchains often use advanced consensus mechanisms, such as Proof-of-Stake or Proof-of-Authority, to minimize energy consumption. Additionally, they may prioritize the use of renewable energy sources for their operations.

By embracing sustainability and environmental responsibility, the cryptocurrency industry can contribute to a more sustainable future.

10. Regulatory Developments

Governments worldwide are creating frameworks to regulate cryptocurrency.

Key Focus Areas:

- **Anti-Money Laundering (AML) and Know Your Customer (KYC) Requirements:** Many countries are implementing stricter AML/KYC regulations for

cryptocurrency exchanges and other digital asset service providers. This aims to prevent illicit activities like money laundering and terrorist financing.
- **Taxation of Crypto Earnings:** Governments are developing tax policies to address the taxation of cryptocurrency gains and losses. This includes capital gains taxes, income taxes, and other relevant levies.
- **Defining Legal Frameworks for DeFi and NFTs:** As DeFi and NFTs continue to grow, regulators are grappling with how to classify and regulate these innovative technologies.

Why It Matters:

- **Regulatory Clarity:** Clear and consistent regulations can provide a stable and predictable environment for the cryptocurrency industry, attracting more institutional investors and mainstream adoption.
- **Consumer Protection:** Regulations can help protect consumers from fraud, scams, and other risks associated with the cryptocurrency market.
- **Innovation and Economic Growth:** A well-regulated crypto industry can foster innovation and drive economic growth.

Emerging Trend: Global Collaboration on Crypto Regulations

Many countries are working together to develop a coordinated approach to crypto regulation. This international collaboration can help ensure consistent standards and avoid regulatory arbitrage.

As the cryptocurrency industry continues to evolve, it's crucial to stay informed about the latest regulatory developments. By understanding the regulatory landscape, you can navigate the complexities of the crypto world and make informed decisions.

WTF Does It All Mean?

The trends shaping cryptocurrency today will define its future. By staying informed and adaptable, you can identify opportunities, make smarter decisions, and position yourself as a knowledgeable participant in the crypto ecosystem.

In the next chapter, we'll discuss "Taking Your First Steps," summarizing what you've learned and helping you put it into action. We'll provide practical tips for getting started, from setting up a wallet to making your first investment.

Pro Tip: Follow trusted news sources, engage with the crypto community, and keep experimenting with new tools and platforms to stay ahead of the curve. Remember, the crypto landscape is constantly evolving, so continuous learning is essential.

Chapter 8:

Taking Your First Steps

Congratulations on Completing Your Foundation

You've reached an important milestone in your crypto journey. By now, you've learned the basics of cryptocurrency, how to set up a wallet, make your first purchase, and stay safe. You've also explored use cases and trends shaping the industry. Now, it's time to turn knowledge into action.

In this chapter, we'll guide you through actionable steps to start engaging with the crypto ecosystem confidently. Whether you're a beginner or an experienced investor, these tips will help you navigate the crypto world with ease.

Let's take the next step together. Remember, every journey starts with a single step, and your crypto journey is no different

1. Set Clear Goals

Before diving deeper into the crypto world, take a moment to define your objectives. What do you hope to achieve with cryptocurrency?

Common Goals:

- **Investing:** Build a diversified portfolio of cryptocurrencies and tokens to potentially generate long-term wealth.
- **Learning:** Explore the underlying technology and use cases of blockchain to gain a deeper understanding of the industry.
- **Using Crypto:** Experiment with using cryptocurrencies for everyday payments, decentralized finance (DeFi), or non-fungible tokens (NFTs).
- **Building:** Contribute to the development of blockchain projects as a developer, designer, or entrepreneur.

Pro Tip: Your goals may evolve over time. Start with one focus and expand your horizons as you gain more experience and knowledge.

By setting clear goals, you can create a roadmap for your crypto journey and stay focused on your objectives.

2. Practice with Small Steps

It's tempting to dive in headfirst, but starting small allows you to learn without overwhelming yourself or risking significant losses.

Actionable Steps:

- **Fund Your Wallet:** Transfer a small amount of cryptocurrency (e.g., $50 in Bitcoin or Ethereum) to

your wallet. This will help you get familiar with the process of sending and receiving funds.
- **Make a Payment:** Try sending cryptocurrency to a friend or paying for a service that accepts crypto. This will give you hands-on experience with using crypto for real-world transactions.
- **Explore DeFi:** Stake a small amount of crypto on a decentralized exchange or lend it on a DeFi platform. This will allow you to earn passive income and learn about the DeFi ecosystem.
- **Experiment with NFTs:** Buy a low-cost NFT to understand the process of buying, selling, and collecting digital assets.

Pro Tip: Document your experiences. Tracking what you learn and mistakes you make will help you refine your strategies and avoid repeating errors.

By taking small steps and gradually increasing your involvement, you can build confidence and knowledge in the crypto world. Remember, the journey of a thousand miles begins with a single step.

3. Stay Engaged with the Community

The crypto world thrives on collaboration and shared knowledge. Engaging with the community can help you stay informed, find opportunities, and connect with like-minded individuals.

Where to Start:

- **Telegram and Discord:** Join groups for your favorite projects or general crypto discussions. These platforms offer real-time updates, announcements, and opportunities to interact with developers and other community members.
- **Reddit:** Explore subreddits like r/CryptoCurrency and r/Ethereum for news, discussions, and expert opinions. You can also participate in discussions, ask questions, and share your insights.
- **Twitter:** Follow key figures, project accounts, and analysts on Twitter for real-time updates and breaking news. You can also engage with other users and participate in crypto-related conversations.
- **Meetups and Conferences:** Attend local or virtual crypto meetups and conferences to network with other enthusiasts, learn from industry experts, and stay updated on the latest trends.

Pro Tip: Participate actively in the community. Ask questions, share your experiences, and contribute to discussions. By being an active member of the community, you can gain valuable insights, build relationships, and help shape the future of the crypto industry.

Remember, the crypto community is a vibrant and diverse ecosystem. By engaging with other members, you can learn from their experiences, share your knowledge, and collaborate on exciting projects.

4. Build Your Learning Routine

The crypto space is dynamic, and continuous learning is essential. Dedicate time to staying updated and expanding your knowledge.

Suggested Resources:

- **News Sites:** Follow reputable news outlets like CoinDesk, CoinTelegraph, and Decrypt for the latest news and analysis.
- **YouTube Channels:** Subscribe to educational channels like Andreas Antonopoulos' channel or those focused on blockchain tutorials and explainers.
- **Podcasts:** Listen to podcasts like Unchained or Bankless for in-depth discussions with industry experts.
- **Books:** Read foundational texts like "The Bitcoin Standard" by Saifedean Ammous or "The Master Algorithm" by Pedro Domingos to gain a deeper understanding of the underlying technologies.
- **Online Courses and Workshops:** Enroll in online courses on platforms like Coursera or Udemy to learn about blockchain development, smart contract programming, or cryptocurrency trading.

Pro Tip: Set a weekly schedule to read, watch, or listen to content that enhances your understanding. Consistent learning will help you stay ahead of the curve and make informed decisions.

By investing time in your education, you can become a more knowledgeable and confident participant in the crypto ecosystem.

5. Expand Your Portfolio Wisely

If investing is one of your goals, consider gradually diversifying your portfolio as you learn more about the market.

Action Plan:

- **Review Your Goals:** Clearly define your investment goals. Are you looking for long-term growth, short-term gains, or exposure to specific trends?
- **Research New Projects:** Explore a variety of cryptocurrencies and blockchain projects, focusing on those with strong fundamentals, experienced teams, and a clear use case.
- **Diversify Your Portfolio:** Spread your investments across different cryptocurrencies to reduce risk. Consider diversifying by market capitalization, asset class, or project stage.
- **Rebalance Periodically:** Regularly review your portfolio and rebalance it as needed to maintain your desired asset allocation.
- **Avoid FOMO (Fear Of Missing Out):** Don't invest in a project simply because it's trending. Conduct thorough research and make informed decisions.

Pro Tip: Avoid over-diversifying. Focus on a few high-quality projects that align with your investment strategy.

By following these guidelines and staying informed, you can build a well-diversified portfolio that can weather market volatility and generate long-term returns.

6. Explore Advanced Use Cases

Once you're comfortable with the basics, challenge yourself by engaging with more advanced aspects of crypto.

Ideas to Explore:

- **Decentralized Autonomous Organizations (DAOs):** Participate in the governance of decentralized organizations by joining a DAO and voting on proposals. This can give you firsthand experience in community-led decision-making.
- **Tokenized Assets:** Explore the world of tokenized assets, such as tokenized real estate or art. This can offer unique investment opportunities and access to previously inaccessible asset classes.
- **Develop on Blockchain:** If you're technically inclined, consider learning to develop dApps or smart contracts. This can be a rewarding and lucrative career path.
- **Yield Farming and Staking:** Earn passive income by providing liquidity to decentralized exchanges or staking your cryptocurrencies to support the network's security.

Pro Tip: Choose one advanced use case and dedicate time to mastering it before moving on. By focusing on a specific area, you can gain deeper knowledge and skills.

Remember, the crypto world is constantly evolving, so stay curious and keep exploring new opportunities. By continuously learning and experimenting, you can unlock the full potential of this exciting technology.

7. Protect Your Gains

As your crypto journey progresses, safeguarding your investments becomes increasingly important.

Key Steps:

- **Use Cold Wallets for Long-Term Storage:** Cold wallets, such as hardware wallets, store your private keys offline, making them highly secure against cyberattacks.
- **Keep Detailed Records:** Maintain accurate records of your transactions, including purchase prices, sale prices, and any associated fees. This will help you track your investments and prepare for tax season.
- **Stay Updated on the Latest Security Threats and Best Practices:** The crypto landscape is constantly evolving, and new security threats emerge regularly. Stay informed about the latest security best practices and implement them to protect your assets.

- **Enable Two-Factor Authentication (2FA):** Enable 2FA on all your exchange and wallet accounts to add an extra layer of security.
- **Be Wary of Phishing Attacks:** Never share your private keys, seed phrases, or other sensitive information with anyone. Be cautious of phishing emails, messages, or websites that may attempt to steal your information.
- **Use Strong, Unique Passwords:** Create strong, unique passwords for each of your crypto accounts and avoid using the same password for multiple accounts.
- **Regularly Update Your Security Software:** Keep your operating system, antivirus software, and other security software up-to-date to protect your devices from malware and other threats.

By following these best practices, you can significantly reduce the risk of losing your cryptocurrency to theft or fraud. Remember, security is an ongoing process, so stay vigilant and adapt your security measures as needed.

8. Reflect and Adjust

Crypto is a journey, not a destination. Take time to reflect on your progress and adjust your strategies as needed.

Questions to Ask Yourself:

- **What have I learned so far?** Assess your knowledge and skills in the crypto space. What areas have you mastered, and where do you need to improve?

- **What challenges have I faced, and how can I overcome them?** Identify any obstacles or setbacks you've encountered and develop strategies to overcome them.
- **What do I want to achieve in the next month, six months, or year?** Set clear, achievable goals and create a plan to reach them.

Pro Tip: Celebrate your wins, no matter how small. Every step forward is progress.

By reflecting on your journey and setting clear goals, you can stay motivated and focused on your crypto endeavors. Remember, the crypto world is constantly evolving, so it's important to stay adaptable and open to new opportunities.

WTF Does It All Mean?

Taking your first steps in crypto can feel daunting, but by starting small, staying informed, and engaging with the community, you'll build the confidence and skills to thrive. Remember, you're not just an observer—you're now a participant in one of the most transformative movements of our time.

In the final chapter, we'll explore "Your Journey Forward," providing motivation and insight into how you can continue to grow and contribute to the crypto ecosystem. We'll discuss the importance of staying curious, seeking out new opportunities, and giving back to the community.

Pro Tip: Take it slow, enjoy the process, and always keep learning. The crypto world is vast, and there's something here for everyone. By approaching your journey with patience and enthusiasm, you can unlock the full potential of this exciting technology.

Chapter 9:

Your Journey Forward

The Beginning of Something Bigger

Congratulations on completing this guide! By now, you've learned how to set up a wallet, make your first crypto purchase, build a portfolio, stay safe, and explore use cases and trends. But this is just the beginning. Your journey in the world of cryptocurrency and blockchain is a continuous process of learning, experimenting, and growing.

In this final chapter, we'll explore how to deepen your engagement with crypto, set meaningful goals, and even contribute to the ecosystem. We'll discuss the importance of community involvement, continuous learning, and ethical considerations.

Remember, the crypto world is constantly evolving, and there's always something new to learn. By embracing this dynamic landscape, you can position yourself as a knowledgeable and active participant in the future of finance and technology.

1. Reflect on What You've Learned

Take a moment to reflect on the key lessons from this guide:

- **Understanding Blockchain and Cryptocurrency:** You've gained a foundational understanding of blockchain technology, its underlying principles, and the various applications of cryptocurrency.
- **Practical Steps:** You've learned how to set up a secure wallet, make your first crypto purchase, and diversify your portfolio.
- **Navigating the Crypto Landscape:** You've explored the dynamic nature of the crypto world, including emerging trends, potential risks, and opportunities.

Ask Yourself:

- **What excited you most about this journey so far?** Was it the potential for financial freedom, the innovative technology, or the community aspect?
- **What areas do you want to explore further?** Are you interested in diving deeper into DeFi, NFTs, or blockchain development?
- **How can you apply what you've learned to your personal or professional life?** Can you use your knowledge to improve your financial literacy, start a side hustle, or contribute to open-source projects?

Pro Tip: Write down your reflections to help clarify your next steps. This will allow you to visualize your goals and track your progress.

By taking the time to reflect on your learning journey, you can gain valuable insights and set the stage for future growth and exploration.

2. Set Long-Term Goals

Now that you've taken your first steps, it's time to think about where you want to go. Cryptocurrency offers a wide range of opportunities, from investing to building and learning.

Possible Goals:

- **As an Investor:**
    - Build a diversified portfolio of cryptocurrencies and tokens.
    - Explore passive income opportunities like staking and lending.
    - Stay updated on market trends and emerging projects.

- **As a Builder:**
    - Learn to code smart contracts and build dApps.
    - Contribute to open-source blockchain projects.
    - Start your own blockchain-based business or project.

- **As a Learner:**
  - Deepen your understanding of blockchain technology and its underlying principles.
  - Explore advanced topics like cryptography, consensus mechanisms, and network security.
  - Stay updated on the latest research and developments in the field.

Pro Tip: Break down your goals into short-term (next 3 months), medium-term (next year), and long-term (5 years or more) objectives. This will help you stay focused and motivated as you work towards your goals.

By setting clear and achievable goals, you can create a roadmap for your crypto journey and track your progress over time. Remember, the most important thing is to enjoy the process and learn from your experiences.

3. Explore Advanced Opportunities

The crypto space is full of opportunities for those willing to dive deeper. Consider these next steps:

- **Participate in a DAO:** Join a Decentralized Autonomous Organization (DAO) to contribute to community-led projects and decision-making processes. DAOs offer a unique way to engage with the crypto community and shape the future of blockchain technology.

- **Stake Your Crypto:** Earn passive income by staking your cryptocurrency on platforms like Ethereum 2.0 or Solana. Staking helps secure the network and rewards participants with additional tokens.
- **Experiment with dApps:** Explore the world of decentralized applications (dApps) and interact with them to gain firsthand experience. dApps offer a wide range of functionalities, from decentralized finance to gaming and social media.
- **Learn to Build on Blockchain:** If you're technically inclined, consider learning to write smart contracts or develop dApps. There are numerous resources available online, including tutorials, courses, and developer communities.

Pro Tip: Take advantage of free online resources, hackathons, and community events to learn and grow. By actively participating in the crypto community, you can connect with like-minded individuals, collaborate on projects, and stay up-to-date with the latest trends.

Remember, the crypto space is constantly evolving, and there are always new opportunities to explore. By staying curious, experimenting, and learning from others, you can unlock the full potential of this exciting technology.

4. Give Back to the Community

The crypto ecosystem thrives on collaboration and community. Sharing your knowledge and experiences can help others and strengthen your own understanding.

Ways to Contribute:

- **Educate Others:** Write articles, create videos, or host workshops to help beginners learn about cryptocurrency and blockchain technology. Sharing your knowledge can help others make informed decisions and avoid common pitfalls.
- **Support Open-Source Projects:** Contribute to the development of open-source blockchain projects by coding, testing, or providing feedback. Your contributions can help improve the security, scalability, and functionality of these projects.
- **Mentor Others:** Share your knowledge and experience with friends, family, or online communities. Mentoring others can be a rewarding experience and help you solidify your own understanding.
- **Participate in Online Forums and Communities:** Engage in discussions on platforms like Reddit, Twitter, and Discord. Share your insights, answer questions, and collaborate with other crypto enthusiasts.

Pro Tip: Even small contributions, like answering questions in online forums or providing feedback on a project, can make a big difference. By actively participating in the community, you can help create a more inclusive and supportive ecosystem.

By giving back to the community, you can help foster a more knowledgeable and vibrant crypto ecosystem. Remember, the more we share, the more we all benefit.

5. Stay Informed and Adaptive

The crypto space moves quickly, with new projects, trends, and challenges emerging every day. Staying informed is essential to staying ahead.

How to Stay Updated:

- **Follow Trusted News Sources:** Keep up with the latest news and developments by following reputable crypto news outlets like CoinDesk, CoinTelegraph, and The Block.
- **Subscribe to Newsletters and Podcasts:** Sign up for newsletters from industry leaders and listen to podcasts that cover crypto topics, such as Unchained or Bankless.
- **Join Online Communities:** Participate in online forums and communities like Reddit, Twitter, and Discord to connect with other crypto enthusiasts and stay updated on the latest trends.
- **Attend Industry Events:** Attend conferences, meetups, and webinars to network with other professionals and learn from industry experts.

Regularly Review Your Portfolio and Strategies

- **Rebalance Your Portfolio:** Periodically review your portfolio and rebalance it to maintain your desired asset allocation.
- **Stay Updated on Market Trends:** Keep an eye on market trends and adjust your investment strategy accordingly.
- **Adapt to Changing Regulations:** Stay informed about the latest regulatory developments and adjust your strategies to comply with relevant laws and regulations.

Pro Tip: Set aside time weekly to catch up on news and deepen your understanding of specific topics. This consistent learning will help you stay ahead of the curve and make informed decisions.

By staying informed and adaptable, you can navigate the ever-changing crypto landscape and position yourself for long-term success.

6. Prepare for Challenges

The road ahead won't always be smooth. The crypto market is known for its volatility, and the technology itself is still evolving.

Common Challenges:

- **Market Volatility:** Cryptocurrency prices can fluctuate significantly in short periods, making it difficult to predict future price movements.

- **Regulatory Uncertainty:** Governments around the world are still developing regulations for the cryptocurrency industry. These regulations can have a significant impact on the market and individual investors.
- **Security Risks:** The decentralized nature of blockchain technology makes it susceptible to various security threats, such as hacking and phishing attacks.
- **Technical Complexity:** Understanding the underlying technology can be challenging, and keeping up with the latest developments requires constant learning.

Pro Tip: Focus on your long-term goals and don't let short-term fluctuations derail your progress. By staying informed, diversifying your portfolio, and practicing sound risk management, you can navigate the challenges and capitalize on the opportunities in the crypto market.

Remember, the crypto space is still relatively new, and it's important to approach it with a long-term perspective. By staying patient, adaptable, and informed, you can position yourself for success in the years to come.

7. Visualize Your Impact

As you grow in the crypto space, think about the broader impact you can have. Blockchain and cryptocurrency are tools for financial inclusion, innovation, and social change.

Questions to Consider:

- **How can I use crypto to solve real-world problems?** Consider supporting projects focused on sustainability, healthcare, or education.
- **What role do I want to play in shaping the future of this technology?** Do you want to become a developer, investor, educator, or community leader?
- **How can I align my crypto journey with my personal values and goals?** Are there specific causes or initiatives that resonate with you?

Pro Tip: Consider joining projects or initiatives that align with your passions. Whether it's contributing to open-source development, participating in a DAO, or supporting a charitable cause, your involvement can make a positive impact.

By visualizing your impact, you can find deeper meaning in your crypto journey and contribute to a more equitable and sustainable future. Remember, the power of blockchain is in the hands of its community, and you can be a part of shaping its destiny.

WTF Does It All Mean?

You've come a long way, but your journey is just beginning. The world of cryptocurrency and blockchain offers endless opportunities to learn, grow, and contribute. Whether you're an investor, builder, or enthusiast, the key is to stay curious, adaptable, and engaged.

As you move forward, remember:

- **Start small but think big:** Begin with achievable goals and gradually expand your horizons.
- **Stay informed and proactive:** Keep up with the latest trends and developments in the crypto space.
- **Give back to the community:** Share your knowledge and experience with others to help foster a thriving ecosystem.

The future of crypto is unwritten, and your actions today can help shape what's next. Embrace the challenges, celebrate the victories, and continue to learn and grow.

Pro Tip: Stay connected to your goals and embrace the challenges as part of the adventure. The possibilities are limitless—so go explore them.

Congratulations on taking the first step! The crypto journey is exciting and rewarding. By staying committed to learning, experimenting, and contributing, you can unlock your full potential and make a lasting impact on the future of technology and finance.

Bonus Material:

Motivation For Your Mission

You Are Part of a Revolution

Take a moment to appreciate the magnitude of what you're now a part of. Cryptocurrency and blockchain technology are reshaping the global financial system, democratizing access to wealth, and redefining how people interact with technology. By engaging with this space, you're not just an observer—you're a participant in a movement that's breaking barriers and building a better future.

As you continue your journey, remember that you're part of a global community of innovators and problem-solvers. Connect with others, share your knowledge, and collaborate on projects that can make a real difference in the world. The future of finance, technology, and society is being shaped by blockchain, and you have the opportunity to be a part of it.

The Power of First Movers

Imagine what it was like to be part of the early days of the internet—when few could grasp its transformative potential. That's where cryptocurrency and blockchain are today. By taking these first steps now, you're positioning yourself as a first mover in an industry poised for explosive growth.

Remember: The actions you take today—learning, experimenting, and building—will pay dividends in the future. You're not late; you're early.

As a first mover, you'll have unique opportunities to:

- **Shape the Future:** Contribute to the development of new technologies and standards.
- **Gain First-Mover Advantage:** Capitalize on early adoption and establish a strong position in the market.
- **Build Valuable Networks:** Connect with other early adopters and industry leaders.

By embracing the challenges and opportunities of this emerging technology, you can become a pioneer in the world of cryptocurrency and blockchain.

Mistakes Are Part of the Process

It's normal to feel overwhelmed or even intimidated by the complexity of crypto. But here's the truth: everyone makes mistakes when they start. What matters is that you learn from them and keep moving forward.

Mindset Shift:

- **Every mistake is a learning opportunity:** Embrace mistakes as a chance to grow and improve your understanding.
- **Every challenge is a chance to grow stronger:** Overcoming obstacles will build your resilience and determination.
- **Every success, no matter how small, is a step toward your ultimate goal:** Celebrate your achievements, no matter how minor they may seem.

Pro Tip: Celebrate your progress. Did you successfully buy your first cryptocurrency? Did you set up a wallet? Each step counts—recognize how far you've come.

Remember, the crypto journey is a marathon, not a sprint. Take your time, be patient, and enjoy the process. By embracing challenges, learning from mistakes, and celebrating your successes, you'll build a strong foundation for your crypto future.

Imagine the Future You're Building

Close your eyes and envision where you want to be in 5 or 10 years:

- **Financial Independence:** Imagine using cryptocurrency to achieve your personal or professional goals. Perhaps you'll have a diversified investment portfolio, generate

- passive income through staking or lending, or even start your own crypto business.
- **Impactful Contributions:** Picture yourself building or contributing to projects that solve real-world problems. You might develop innovative dApps, support sustainable initiatives, or create art and music on the blockchain.
- **Global Citizenship:** Think about how you're part of a borderless, decentralized movement connecting people worldwide. You can collaborate with others from different cultures, share knowledge, and contribute to a more equitable future.

The steps you take today are paving the way for that future. Stay focused, inspired, and committed to your goals. Remember, the crypto journey is a marathon, not a sprint. By taking consistent steps and learning from your experiences, you can achieve your dreams and make a positive impact on the world.

The Ripple Effect of Your Actions

Your crypto journey doesn't exist in a vacuum. The knowledge and experience you gain have the potential to impact others. Whether it's helping a friend set up their first wallet or inspiring a new generation of builders, your actions create a ripple effect that extends far beyond yourself.

Consider:

- How can you help others understand and benefit from cryptocurrency?
    - Share your knowledge and experiences with friends, family, and online communities.
- What unique skills or perspectives can you bring to the table?
    - Are you a talented developer, a skilled writer, or a passionate advocate for financial inclusion?
- How can your story inspire others to take their first steps?
    - Share your successes, failures, and lessons learned to motivate others to embark on their own crypto journey.

Pro Tip: Share your journey. Write about your experiences, host a workshop, or create content to demystify crypto for others.

By sharing your knowledge and inspiring others, you can help build a more informed and empowered crypto community. Remember, the future of cryptocurrency depends on the collective efforts of individuals like you.

What Great Things Start With

Every great innovation starts with small, courageous steps:

- The first email sent.
- The first website launched.
- The first Bitcoin transaction.

You're now part of that legacy. Each time you learn something new, take action, or inspire someone else, you're contributing to the growth of this revolutionary ecosystem. Small steps lead to big changes—trust the process.

As you continue your crypto journey, remember that you're part of a global community of innovators and pioneers. Connect with others, share your knowledge, and collaborate on projects that can shape the future. By embracing the challenges and opportunities of the crypto world, you can make a positive impact and leave a lasting legacy.

You're Not Alone

It's easy to feel like you're navigating uncharted waters, but the truth is, the crypto community is filled with people just like you: curious, motivated, and eager to learn. Lean on the community for support, insights, and collaboration.

Motivational Reminder:

- **There's a network of people rooting for you to succeed.** Don't be afraid to reach out to others for help and advice.

- **Every question you have is valid.** Don't be afraid to ask questions, no matter how basic they may seem.
- **Every effort you make moves you forward.** Even small steps can lead to significant progress.

Pro Tip: Find a mentor or accountability partner to share your journey with. Having someone to support and encourage you can make a big difference.

Remember, the crypto community is a diverse and welcoming place. By connecting with other like-minded individuals, you can learn from their experiences, share your knowledge, and build lasting relationships.

Your Potential Is Limitless

The most exciting thing about your crypto journey is that it's entirely your own. You have the freedom to:

- **Explore new technologies:** Dive deep into the world of blockchain, decentralized finance, and NFTs.
- **Create meaningful projects:** Build your own dApps, contribute to open-source projects, or start your own crypto business.
- **Build wealth and independence:** Invest in promising projects, earn passive income through staking or lending, and secure your financial future.

Motivational Mantra:

- "I am learning."

- "I am growing."
- "I am shaping the future."

As you continue your journey, remember that the possibilities are endless. Embrace the challenges, celebrate the victories, and never stop learning. You have the power to make a real impact on the world.

A Final Call to Action

The crypto world isn't waiting for someone else to lead—it's waiting for you. Take the knowledge you've gained, the skills you've built, and the vision you've cultivated, and go create something extraordinary.

Remember:

- **You don't have to have it all figured out today.** Start with small steps and build on your successes.
- **Progress, not perfection, is the goal.** Don't let fear of failure hold you back. Embrace challenges as opportunities to learn and grow.
- **The future of crypto is being written by people like you—dreamers, doers, and believers.** Your actions today can shape the future of technology and finance.

This is your journey, your adventure, and your time to shine. Go make it happen.

The future of cryptocurrency and blockchain is bright, and you have the potential to be a part of it. So, take the leap, embrace the unknown, and let your crypto journey begin.

Thanks for reading,

Jason Ansell

www.ingramcontent.com/pod-product-compliance
Lightning Source LLC
Chambersburg PA
CBHW071023240526
45469CB00006BD/2054